Life on Brier Island
Nova Scotia

Stories and Photos
About the Place
the People and the Boats

Caroline B. Norwood

Canadian Cataloguing in Publication Data

Norwood, Caroline B.
  Life on Brier Island

    ISBN 0-9698310-1-3
1. Brier Island (N.S.) —History. 2. Brier Island
(N.S.) —Biography. 1. Title.

FC2345.B74N67 1995   971.6'32   C95-950135-5
F1039.B74N67 1995

Cover Photo - The Titus Lady haddock trawling in the Bay of Fundy,
1993. L. to r. Chris Titus, Lindsay Titus, and Capt. Pete Titus.
Title page photo: That Girl owned by Clyde Titus.
Back cover photo: Western Light sunset by Thomas E. Norwood.

Copyright, 1995 by Caroline B. Norwood
Norwood Publishing, P.O. Box 1192, Westport, Nova Scotia
BOV 1HO

Copies available from the Publisher
 Printed in Canada on recycled archival quality paper by
Sentinel Printing Limited, Yarmouth, N.S. B5A 1S7

Contents

On the Waterfront

Memorable Island Meetings and Other Stories

Illustrations

Illustrations

Illustrations

Illustrations

Illustrations

Albert Moore helps on Dumping Day
Weighing lobsters at the Pound
Roger Thomas at the Pound
Trevor Frost at the Lobster Point
Clyde Titus with the sunken That Girl
First Slocum Tidal Race
Winners of the Slocum Middy Race
Wilbur "Dube" Frost and the Elaine Gail
Bringing in the battered TamTan
Henry Porter at the helm
Former Coast Guard building
Winston McCullough on the **CG 102**
Capt. Evan McDormand and crew, Marty McDormand
Marty and Evan in 1978
Martin & Evan I
RayMcDormand and the **Martin & Evan II**
Marty and Evan with giant lobster;
Capt. Glendon Titus on the **Spray;** Petite Passage ferry
Ferry **Grand Passage**
Island Princess
Kenney plant in winter; And in the summer
Danny Kenney
Pete Titus on the **Just Four**
Night view of Kenney transport truck
Russian factory ship
Doraine B. on the rocks Being pulled from the rocks
Titus Lady heads out with traps
Timberwind fueling up;
Fundy Gypsy and the **Little Spitter;Wanda Lou**
Western Light seen from **Fundy Gypsy**
The **Mr. Jake**
Lightkeeper's dwelling torn down
The ferry **Spray**
The ferry **Joshua Slocum**
Wanda Graham and Becky shopping

Illustrations

Protest Teacher cut
Getting together for Thanksgiving
Westport from the High Knoll, 1920
Sunday School class in the Baptist Church
Alva McDormand shoots a moose
View of Brier Island Lodge
Four accidents
Frank Norwood practicing basketball
Skating on Lively's Pond
Gordy Gets Some Help With Sign
Two old schools - Westport and Freeport
The old hearse
Ross Anderson banding birds
Super Seniors in the Westport Convention Parade
Westport Public Library
School children sing at Grand Opening
Betty Shea presents clock
Westport School in 1979
Plant workers arrive in Westport on ferry
Tom Cat Alley
Nancy Swift at the Westport Inn

A view of the southern end of Grand Passage showing Peters Island Light and Long Island from Green Head on the southern shore of Brier Island, 1989. Photo by Thomas E. Norwood.

Jake and Madeline Dixon

Karyn and Hayden Norwood

Introduction

I came to live in Westport on Brier Island in late August, 1976. I arrived in a yellow compact stationwagon with husband and six children. The oldest child, Dan, was 14 The youngest, Susanna, was nine weeks. My husband, Laforest (Huck) Norwood had just gotten the job of teaching principal at the Westport School. We had been living in Pubnico for two years. Before that, we lived in Maine where my husband had a fish dragger and also taught school.

I remember well the long trip from our home in Pubnico. There was the first ferry at East Ferry. Then a very winding road behind a car moving along at 40 mph. Finally, the second ferry which at that time was a strange looking contraption people jokingly called the Yellow Submarine.

We stopped at the Co-op Store and asked about houses for sale. Maureen Swift was working at the checkout. She sent us back to see Wilfred Swift, the manager. He looked out his office window and gestured toward a huge, rather rundown looking place in the next yard. He said he thought we could get that place at a reasonable price.We bought the house and moved in a few days later. We've been here ever since. My husband only taught school for three years. Then he became a lighthouse keeper. Then he retired.

Four of our children have stayed in the area. Daughter Charlotte married Vance Dixon from Tiverton. They live nearby with children Jake and Madeline. Dan built a house near the Baptist Church where he lives with his wife, Marlene Welch, a Westport native. Susanna, now 18, lives with us. Son Thomas recently married Nichole Titus from Westport. They live in Yarmouth, N.S. Two of our sons decided to live in the USA. Frank lives in Keene, N.H. with wife Tonnya and children ,Karyn and Hayden. Nelson has lived in Tampa. Fla. for the past 10 years. For my husband and I, after many years of moving up and down the Maine coast feel we have finally found a place to call home, Brier Island.

I've always written stories so I kept right on after I moved here. Many of the stories herein were first published in The Digby Courier while I was editor of that newspaper. The date on each story indicates when it was published or when the person was interviewed. I believe every individual has an interesting story to tell.

Each person's life is unique and we can benefit from learning about the experiences of other people.I offer many views of Brier Island. Interviews with longtime residents; photos and stories about fishing boats and their owners and reports from important meetings from years past. Life is changing for those who live on Brier Island. With this book,I attempt to preserve a bit of Brier Island history and also give a glimpse of what the future may hold.

Caroline B.Norwood
Westport, Brier Island, Nova Scotia, Canada
February 1, 1995

The Place....

A view of Westport in the early 1900's. This is the area just before the High Knoll. Photo courtesy Florence Denton

An American's Impressions
of Westport in 1934

This article was first printed in **The Digby Weekly Courier** *Sept. 14, 1934. It is an account written by a visitor from Massachusetts.*

We are now at our last port of call in Nova Scotia - Westport - a tiny fishing village on the extreme tip of Digby Neck, and, as we were told, the nearest point in Nova Scotia to the United States.Two ferries were used to bring us to this island, which is the second inhabited one from the mainland.

At Tiverton, we met "By" Blackford, who is probably better known to American tourists than any other three men in the provinces.he has been ferrying automobiles across the treacherous stretch of water between Digby Neck and Long Island for the past 42 years, ever since he was 19 years old.

"By" has an inexhaustible store of stories and jokes. He is always willing to dig into it for the amusement of his customers.The second ferry plies between Freeport and Westport; and its pilot and owner, a Mr. Morrell, is similarly equipped with yarns.my car, he said, was the first to be ferried to Westport in nearly two weeks and its arrival was sufficiently unusual to collect a crowd of nearly 50 persons.

Westport's homes are straggled around the bay with only a road and breastworks separating the houses from the water. Piers extend into the water in all directions and a sizable collection of fishing boats is anchored just off the shore.

Directly in front of me, as I type this, is a weir, not more than 50 yards from the front lawn of the home at which we are stopping. Yesterday, the weir captured a "horse mackerel" or as it is better known, a tuna.It was nearly two hours before the weir's owners were able to kill the fish which weighed nearly 750 pounds. Harpoons and fishforks were called into play before it was sufficiently subdued to be towed to a wharf where its head was cut off.

The tuna appeared about 8 feet long and was nearly as thick through its body as it was long. As I write this, I am convinced fishing holds no more thrills for me. I've caught a shark, and not a "mackerel shark" either, but the variety that are not at all adverse to sampling human flesh. Furthermore, I hooked it with a small pollock line. Lloyd Denton, at whose home I am staying and who has taken us on some of his regular fishing trips, was responsible for landing the ugly-looking, furious fish.

I held the line while he stabbed it repeatedly with a long gaff.It was still alive and lunging or sheering as they call it here, when Mr. Denton and I hauled it on the stern of the boat.Eventually,and it did not seem nearly soon enough, the fish was shoved back into the water where it circled around the boat for nearly an hour before finally disappearing.Mr. Denton assured me that it was highly unusual to hook and bring a shark alongside a boat with only a light line.

He attributed it to the fact that the hook had lodged in a corner of the shark's mouth where it was unable to bite off the line.Fishermen here, I was told, frequently lose hooks and weights when a shark takes hold, and it is not out of the ordinary to have them bite through big ropes or even to sever wire leads.Sharks are hunted only for sport and apparently serve no useful purpose. Mine weighed about 170 pounds and was about seven feet long.Last year a whale was beached near here and sharks followed it for food.Westport fishermen harpooned many of them and one was brought ashore.To all appearances the fish was dead and men and boys were pulling the teeth for souvenirs.

The teeth were nearly all extracted when the shark suddenly revived, flopped down the beach and into the water where it swam away.You don't have to believe it but every other person in Westport will verify the story.But we were out for pollock and not sharks and later in the day we caught many of them, 94 to be exact and weighing about 1,000 pounds.Waters hereabouts abound in fish although August is considered an off month for them.

There are four popular methods of fishing here. They are known as drailing, plugging, tiding and trawling.Tiding is the most economical and so far, has been productive of the greatest number of fish. The fisherman goes out just before flood tide and anchors his boat off the ledge or shoals where he knows the fish feed.As the tide goes out, the water rushes past his boat and carries the lines out to sea.

The lines are attached to outriggings and are less weighted and longer on the outside than those nearer the boat.A fish is hooked by

The D & D Grill on Water Street, owned by Dougie and Debbie De-laney. Photo by Thomas E. Norwood

Irishtown in the early 1900's. Photo courtesy Florence Denton

Five generations in the family of Digby County Warden Wilfred Swift gathered for a family photo in Westport last week. Shown standing, l. to r. are Warden Swift, his son, Roland Lewis; seated, his mother, Geneva; granddaughter, Dana Smith and great-granddaughter, Leah Nicole Smith, age four weeks.(1980)

Enjoying a warm spring day. l. to r. Janet MacLauchlan, Lorainne Bezant and Barbara McDormand. (1993)

Gathering bait at Sweet Cake Cove in Irishtown, early 1900's.Photo by Albert Morrel, courtesy Mary Graham.

the flow of the tide when it bites at the bait and it is simply a matter of pulling it in.only pollock are caught by tiding and the fish are game enough to put up a sharp struggle as they are hauled near the boat. Drailing would be recognized in the States as trolling. Lines are hung over the side of the boat and the motor set at a low speed.the fish are harder to land, since the forward motion of the boat increases the amount of pull on the line.plugging is a still more arduous method, chiefly used for cod, since it involves constantly throwing out the line and weight and hauling it in.

Trawl fishing consists of sinking a long line to which 100 or more small lines and hooks are attached. The trawl is "run" at regular intervals and fish are removed from the lines attached to the long one. Halibut are frequently caught this way.

Social Convention

There is a social convention in Westport which, apparently, even summer visitors must observe.every clear Saturday night, at 7 o'clock sharp, natives and visitors dress up and parade slowly up and down the main street until 8 o'clock when it is permitted to return home or to go to the town's solitary weekly movie.dressing up involves a suit, complete with coat and vest, one cap and a shave.

Nearly everyone is out walking at that time. Men collect outside the few stores, while women-folk enjoy themselves with Saturday shopping. Girls stroll in giggling groups of three and four and young men and boys congregate in the shadows of wharf buildings to comment in scarcely audible asides on the parade.

Because there are no street lights, the walk ends at dark. A majority move off to the town's only other important street which is graced by a school, Oddfellow's Hall and residence, to attend the theatre, while others turn toward their various homes.the movie showing was "The Singing Fool" with Al Jolson but was unfortunately lacking in the equipment to make it audible.

Church circles and fraternal organizations make up the chief social activity in Westport and the show's only competition as an amusement centre is infrequent dances, music for which is furnished by local talent. Oh, yes, there are also baseball games, although a good run of fish, fog or storms often causes their postponement.Saturday evening . I watched a loudly-cheering, victorious nine return home.

The team, plus the fans it had brought with them, were packed solidly into a fishing boat which was ploughing noisily and triumphantly across the bay.I hope I have not given the impression that Westport is a dull place. It is anything but that. The people here are friendly and hospitable to an extreme and take a genuine and kindly interest in the entertainment of their infrequent guests.In all the towns I have visited in Nova Scotia, I have found none more charming than this one.

Tourists, I suppose, will eventually "discover" it and make of it, like Digby, a place of summer hotels, overnight cabins, hooked rug stands and tearooms. I hope the day is far off. In the meantime, I've found a place which I hope to return to often.

Editors Note: The next story shows how much things changed from 1934 to 1980.The fish weirs were gone; the movie theatre torn down to make way for a public library. There was no bus to carry passengers from Tiverton to Freeport. The waterfront had changed tremendously because of the Feb. 2,1976, Groundhog Storm.

An aerial view of Westport, showing the Baptist Church

Swimming in Westport Harbour, June 6, 1980 -l . to r. Cheryl Titus, Charlotte Norwood ,i n front,Susanna Norwood.

A view of Water Street in the early 1900's. House shown was the John Churchill residence and was an ice cream parlour. The picket fence is in front of the house now occupied by Theresa and Danny Kenney. Photo courtesy Florence Denton

An aerial view of Westport taken in the 1940's.
Photo courtesy of Donald Glavin

On Jan. 17, 1980, drift ice appeared in Westport Harbour. This was unusual because ice normally arrives in late February or March. The drifting ice did not hamper the ten fishermen still lobstering from West port but did delay ferry crossings.

Village Life in
Westport, Nova Scotia
First published in the **Canadian Geographic**,
Feb./Mar 1980

On a foggy day, standing on the hill overlooking the Village of
Westport on Brier Island in Nova Scotia, you can hear three separate
fog horns; the distinct moans from Peters Island Light, Grand Passage
Light and Brier Island Light. Peters Island dominates the entrance to
the harbour from St. Mary's Bay. Grand Passage Light is now a modern
tripod affair. It sounds the alarm at the east side of the wide mouth of
the Bay of Fundy. Brier Island Light, a traditional red-and-white
striped sentinel, guards the southwestern side of Brier Island.

Below the hill, 350 people go about their lives on this 4-by-1-1/2
mile rocky island. A fisherman wends his way in his pickup truck from
his home at one end of Water Street to his boat near the other end. His
big black dog rides in back. You can follow the progress of the truck by
listening to other dogs barking at the passing black rider.The whine of
two Caterpillar engines on the 12-car ferry signifies the arrival of this
moving link between Brier Island and Long Island. If the ferry is on
schedule, it will be about 12 minutes past the hour. At 25 past the hour,
the engines turn over again and the boat starts on its way back to the slip
in Freeport on Long Island, a trip of scarcely a mile.

Westport was aptly named. It is the port of the most westerly part of
Nova Scotia. It is also on the western side of Grand Passage, the watery
thoroughfare separating Brier Island from Long Island. With Grand
Manan Island, N.B., it guards the waters entering the Bay of Fundy.

The island was named after a Captain Brier who stopped here for
water in the late 1600's. The next recorded visitor was Joshua Welch
who came here from Maine in 1763 to try the fishing. It was great.
Other fishermen soon followed, including his son, David and Robert
Morrell. Twenty years later, 11 Loyalist families moved here bearing
such surnames as Buckman, Payson, Sullivan, Coggins, Lafoldy, Bailey
and Denton.

Fishing continues to be the mainstay of the island. About 27 boats
fish for lobster during the Nov. 28-May 31 season. During the rest of
the year, some men fish for herring. Others set trawls for halibut and

hake or they jig for haddock, cod, pollock and squid; and, of course, they work at the fish houses or sheds where they store and mend their nets, traps and other gear. There is one fish firm, the rapidly expanding D.B. Kenney employs 38 people in the summer and 12 year-round. Kenney's maintains the only lobster pound on the island, with a capacity of 50,000 pounds of live lobsters. It handles salt and fresh fish, scallops and lobsters. The company also has the only heavy equipment machinery in the area. It does the snow plowing for the island people.

There are only 10 miles of road, four paved, six gravel-surfaced, and there are no traffic lights. Bicycles are popular with all ages. Children ride by, wearing hip boots. A dignified man may pedal along sedately, holding a large whole haddock in one hand. A middle-aged woman rings the bell on her adult tricycle as she wheels her way to the post office.

Paved roads run the length of the village around an L-shaped harbour and up to the hilltop to the cemetery. The main section of the village contains two general stores, two churches, the school, ferry landing, Coast Guard station, fish plant, and various small wharves and fish houses.

Where the L-shaped road turns, there is a large culvert running under it. This drains a wide, marshy area known as Big Meadow. People who live beyond the culvert (known as "the bridge") are said to live in Irish Town. This section was so named because Irish families first settled the area. Tillis, Casey, Margeson and Welsh were some of the first residents.

The local authority on island history says that "traditionally the poorer families lived in Irish Town where the soil was thin. The 'aristocrats' lived on the other side of the bridge in Snob Town, under the hill where there was thick rich soil. In Irish Town, a family had one cow; in Snob Town, they'd have two."

Today, anyone going in the direction of Irish Town will say he is going "down" the road. Going from Irish Town, one goes "up" the road. "Up" the road are the Baptist Church and the Church of Christ. Then there is the old Westport High School which once had classes from primary through to Grade 12. It is now owned by an American. Next to the old school is a dome-shaped recreation hall and an attached garage for two fire trucks. This was completed in 1977.

Adjoining the recreation hall is the Westport Public Library, a $45,000 building completed in 1978 under a Canada Works grant. A province-wide appeal for used books brought nearly 4,000 volumes to the island. Bingo is played every Friday evening at the Odd Fellows Hall, next to the library. The hall was built in 1910 with lumber salvaged from the ship Aurora which went ashore here at Cow Cove in 1908. School musical productions are presented in the hall, the only building in town with a stage.

The present Westport School is on the Back Road, a paved road which parallels Water Street through the centre of the village. There are four teachers for about 60 pupils enrolled in grades from primary through to Grade 8. After Grade 8, students take the 8:25 a.m. ferry each weekday to Freeport. They are met at the ferry landing by a bus which takes them to Islands Consolidated in Freeport, a primary-to-grade 12 school serving both Long and Brier Islands.

The two stores provide most of the necessities of life. One is a co-op, the other R.E. Robicheau, Ltd., a family-run general store. Robicheau's also has gas pumps and carries plumbing and building supplies in addition to groceries, dry goods and hardware.

Though the stores do provide necessities, customers have to wait for some items. Fresh fruit and produce come by truck every Tuesday afternoon from Digby. It is wise to get bananas or tomatoes by Wednesday because they are apt to be sold out by Thursday. Milk and bread trucks make tri-weekly visits in summer, biweekly in winter. Meat, ice cream and frozen foods arrive in a noisy refrigerator truck each Tuesday. Atlantic Wholesalers Ltd. , an interprovincial Maritime distributor, delivers canned goods on Wednesdays. The "pop" truck comes only once a month.

The bank also arrives on wheels. The Bank of Nova Scotia maintains a sub-branch in Westport. It leases a tiny waterfront building and sends over money and pertinent bank records from Freeport every Thursday afternoon. Banking hours are 1 p.m. to 4 p.m. You wait your turn on a six-foot bench in front of the window and anyone listening carefully may learn just how much each patron deposits or receives for his or her paycheck.

Actually there aren't many paychecks for "her." The waterfront belongs to the men. Rarely do women accompany men on fishing trips.

They do work in the fish plant during the summer. Two of the four teachers are local women. One woman has worked in the office of the fish plant for 52 years.The only other jobs held by women are two positions as sales clerks in the general stores and one as the part-time postmaster. Westport has a modern brick post office. Mail comes on the 10 a.m. ferry and usually is "put up" by 10:45. The truck departs with outgoing mail on the 12:25 ferry.

Even the garbage leaves on the ferry. In times happily past, people threw their garbage of the breakwater or over the side of the breastwork surrounding the harbour. Now a truck comes over every Monday to remove refuse to a dump near Tiverton at the far end of Long Island.

With so much of island life dependent on the ferry,it is a relief that service is maintained quite well. The boat ties up at Westport after midnight but can be called by a VHF radio transmitter set up at the Freeport landing. Weather seldom necessitates a complete shut-down of service. Occasionally a severe winter storm will bring things to a halt for a day or two but people cope admirably. A spare ferry usually is kept moored in the harbour.In real emergencies, there is always the 44-ft. Coast Guard lifeboat which is kept at the government breakwater. The Coast Guard base and boat are one of four in Nova Scotia. There is a doctor in Freeport with an office in his house. The ambulance is based at a Freeport general store. The 44-mile trip from Freeport to Digby General Hospital includes another short ferry crossing from Tiverton to East Ferry, but, with a good road, the ambulance can make the trip in scarcely an hour.

Digby is the nearest town and shopping area. The cinema, liquor store and hospital are in Digby. The trip to town involves catching the Westport ferry by 25 past the hour, driving 11 miles up Long Island to reach the Tiverton ferry which departs on the hour. The crossing to East Ferry on the mainland takes about four minutes and a further 33-mile drive brings you to Digby.

Faced with this trip in reverse, many tourists forsake the visit to Brier Island, but a few determined people do come every summer.
There are some summer residents but no big estates. Americans own much of the choice waterfront property. As yet there are no "Private-Keep Out" signs; people can walk to the shore anywhere on the island.

Naturalists visit Brier Island specifically to see birds, whales or rocks. The island is an officially-recognized migrating bird stopover point. In the fall, groups of binocular and camera-equipped birdwatchers can be seen trekking up the gravel road toward North Point or wandering along the paths which skirt the island's entire 16-mile circumference.

Another annual group of visitors consists of whale watchers who hire lobster boats to search for whales offshore. Usually the trips are successful. A few years ago, a huge finback whale beached itself here. Its bleached bones are being prepared for display at Toronto's Ontario Science Centre.

Lapidary enthusiasts visit the island to search for agates. The basalt cliffs here are of interest. They are mainly on the south side of the island and resemble stone pillars. Some are 120 ft. high. The columns have been likened to the Giant's Causeway in Northern Ireland.

In recent years, Westport has staked a claim to fame by advertising itself as the "home of Joshua Slocum." Slocum was the first person to circumnavigate the world alone. He was born in Wilmot Township in neighbouring Annapolis County, Feb. 20, 1844. His mother was a Westport native, the daughter of John Suthern. Slocum came to Westport when he was eight and left at the age of 16.

He next visited Brier Island 35 years later on his three-year voyage around the world. He stayed a month while making repairs on his 36-ft., 13-ton sloop, **Spray**. He returned once again, five years later. This time he lingered two months, and while here, read the proofs of his book, Sailing Alone Around the World.

On the strength of these historic facts, the Slocum Society has erected a monument to Slocum at South Point. A local store sells T-shirts emblazoned with a silhouette of Slocum and his ship, featuring the words, "Brier Island,Home of Joshua Slocum." During the short time Slocum did live here, his home was in Irish town.

Life is casual but not uncomplicated in Westport. Social activities consist of church services and church meetings, bingo (here and on Long Island,) playing cards in a neighbor's kitchen, conversations in the co-op, sitting in a fish house and talking, or sitting on the "cement block" at the ferry landing and watching the world go by. Children are free to wander almost anywhere on the island, but usually come home at suppertime when they hear parents calling. You can hear the names being yelled from back steps and the answering, "I'm coming," from "up" or "down" the road.

There are baby showers, occasional weddings, and enough funerals to show that there are more people going than coming. Dances are held in the recreation hall with loud "country western" bands and a busy bar. Each July there are suppers and a "Brier Island Weekend." Naturalists visit Brier Island specifically to see birds, whales or rocks. The island is an officially recognized migrating bird stopover point. In the fall, groups of binocular and camera-equipped birdwatchers can be seen trekking up the gravel road toward North Point or wandering along the paths which skirt the island.

Many people go for evening drives, cruising slowly over the four miles of paved road, from one end of the village to the other and back again. Young people walk the streets, play games at the Recreation Hall when it is open, ride their bikes, and in summer fish or swim in the cold translucent waters.

Children play on piles of lobster traps. One day a group of girls will pretend the traps make a house. Barbie dolls sit on the laths and doll meals are created out of green sea lettuce, choice mussels, periwinkles and dulse. The next day, the traps might form a fort for a group of boys. They will dodge in and out of a three-story stack of traps, shooting driftwood guns at each other.

Many lives are regulated by the tide. Extreme neap tide is 28 ft.; average daily tide is 18 ft. If you are picking dulse or digging clams, you are well aware that the tides move in or out at an average of three feet per hour. The current through the southwest passage tears by at six knots. Slocum referred to this current as "the worst tide-race in the Bay of Fundy." Clearly the movement of the waters surrounding Brier Island is something to be reckoned with.

The picturesque waterfront had remained unchanged for many years until the "Groundhog Day" storm of Feb. 2, 1976. More than 40 waterfront buildings were lost in that short storm. Yet Westport today remains a visually interesting place. Many homes date from the early and mid-1800's. Some of the old fish houses remain, including one where "native son" Joshua Slocum worked as a boy in the 1850's, helping his father to make leather boots for fishermen.

There are usually some 60-80 ft. seine or scallop boats moored in the harbour, as well as the colourfully painted lobster boats. A few yachts may stop for an overnight visit during summer or fall. The scene is always varied as the tide rises and falls, as the sun shines, or -more often- as the fog rolls in.

Snowfall is slight but frequently there is "sea smoke" covering the water (when the air is much colder than the water). Then there are the storm days, when waves break on top of the rock barrier which lines the harbour. Boats toss at their moorings, spray hits the windows of waterfront houses. This is Westport, a quiet but interesting place to live.

Near Western Light. Photo by Thomas E. Norwood (1989)

*The Community Hall. This is the former Oddfellow's Hall built with lumber salvaged from the iron sailing barque **Aurora** which came ashore on Brier Island in November, 1908 with one million ft. of lumber.*

Sheltered from the storm. Photo by Thomas E. Norwood

34

A major event: the road is paved on Brier Island
This photo was taken in August, 1988.

Rexie Titus 'Shop, once used by Norman Deviller who repaired shoes
and by Scottie Robertson, a tailor. Scottie allegedly drank Nonesuch
stove polish which he strained through a loaf of bread.

*School children wait to get off the ferry **Spray** as it lands in Freeport. They were going to the waiting bus. 1985*

The ferry heads toward Westport past a string of fishing boats moored in the harbour. (1988)Photo by Thomas E. Norwood

THE PIONEERS OF BRIER ISLAND

By Margaret Armstrong Archibald - written in the 1930's.
Elaine Robertson gave a copy to the Westport Library.

Many books and manuscripts have been written about the pioneers of Nova Scotia, who toiled to improve their lands in the various counties, but not much attention has been paid to those of Digby County and its two islands, Long and Brier, the township of Westport on Brier. It is the westernmost land belonging to N.S. To reach the island, one must first travel from Digby down the length of Digby Neck to East Ferry. Anyone familiar with the map of Nova Scotia will remember the narrow Neck jutting out between St. Mary's Bay and the Bay of Fundy.

The bus leaves Digby each day during the summer, after the passenger trains are in. This bus runs as far as East Ferry. Many tourists go to Sandy Cove, 20 miles from Digby. There is also a good cove on St. Mary's Bay and another on the Bay of Fundy where people may bathe. The distance from Sandy Cove to East Ferry is 10 miles.

Here one crosses Petite Passage, a mile-wide passage, separating Long Island from Digby Neck peninsula. There is a very steep hill to descend from the highway to the beach and one feels safer to walk down it than to ride. On the wharf is a huge iron hoop, suspended by a rope from a beam. Attached to another rope is an iron bar to sound the hoop with. The sound carries across to Tiverton, Long Island, summoning the ferryman, Byron Blackford.

This ferry has been tended by the Blackfords, with two exceptions, ever since 1804, when the General Session granted Martin Blackford the license to run a ferry across Petite. His sons, Anthony, Joseph and Israel, also tended the ferry across Petite, after their father's death. Charles Outhouse and David Scott were two other ferrymen. Henry Aline Blackford was succeeded by his son, Byron, who has been ferryman for over 30 years. Autos are ferried across on a scow, but it is less trouble to motor the 12 miles to Freeport in a small bus run by Edward Blackford, brother of Byron.

At Freeport, one must cross Grand Passage. This channel is wider than Petite and separates Long and Brier islands. George Morrell, son of Robert, an early settler, commenced the ferry between the two islands. This has been carried on by his descendants. Ralph Morrell is the present ferryman. Another ferry was established in 1822 by James Peters, to cross near the southern end of the channel. This ferry was abandoned after a few years. Morrell's track lay between Fish Point Long Island, the Dike on the western side of Grand Passage. Both Blackford and Morrell have fine motor boats with a small cabin for travellers in rough weather.

As the boat approaches Brier Island, one is surprised to see so many gulls circling about. These birds are plentiful because they are protected by law. There are fish cleaning factories along the shore where fish are cleaned for the factory at Freeport. The birds live on fish refuse. Near the shore,the water is literally white with gulls.

It is commonly supposed that the island received its name from one of its settlers, Briar Rice. Others declare that the pioneers named their home after the brambly thickets at the back of the island. The island itself is four miles long and one and one-half wide. It is one of the foremost fishing stations on the western coast. At one time, the population was 800 but so many have emigrated to the United States that today the population is 450.

Most of the people have well-built, comfortable homes and every modern convenience. Nearly every family has a radio, and they are able to enjoy the programs in the long winter months when the mail steamers are often delayed. In summer, mails go through each day, arriving at 8 p.m. In winter, mails take two days.

Horses rest overnight at Sandy Cove. Steamers passing from St.John to Yarmouth call twice a week if the weather is clear. In 1810, Lemuel Morehouse,son of James Morehouse, the Loyalist, accepted a contract to carry mails weekly between Digby and Westport. He distributed the mail at the various houses.

The harbour is off Grand Passage and is almost land surrounded. The northern end of the Passage winds into the Bay of Fundy. At the southern end is a tiny island called Peters Island. The narrow passage either side of it enters St.Mary's Bay. A light house was built on Peters Island in 1850 and remodeled in 1909. John D. Suthern was the first keeper and was given the salary of $100 a year. The Sutherns have always been the keepers of this light.

Brier Island is rocky but has good gravel roads. There are two principal streets, running the length of the island, and parallel to the shore on the Grand Passage side. On a fine day in summer, it is a common sight to see thousands of cod spread out on the flakes along the roadside, to dry. There is a small deserted wharf before nearly every house on the main street, two large wharves being mainly used now.

Westport has two finely equipped lighthouses. The western light was built in 1809. The first keeper was John Suthern Sr. He was succeeded by Joseph Bancroft, John Peters and the present keeper, Albert Welch. A fog alarm was installed at Western Point in 1873. The North Point Lighthouse was built in 1901, Charles Buckman was the first tender and of the Fog Bell operated by machinery, as well.

On the other long street facing the harbour is the Bethel or Disciples of Christ church. It was built in 1859. The first converts were made in 1859 by George Garraty of Milton, Queens County. The minister from Tiverton preaches at this church.

The school house is on this street and is a two storied, well-equipped building. In order that their children might be educated the early settlers paid one of their number to teach the little ones to spell, read, write and do arithmetic. The girls learned to sew beautifully. These were called Dame's schools and were often held at the teacher's house.

The first real schoolhouse was about 20 feet square, and a very primitive style. This was quite a large church. Inside the front entrance were steps on either side leading to the vestry where there were high square pews. After the new church was built, this building was used for Sunday School and later as a part of the small school next to it. As the result of revivals held by the Baptists in 1804,1806, 1809, under Messrs. Towner Crandall and James Manning, there were many converts. In 1810, Peter Crandall baptized 33 persons at Westport, out of 18 families. The first resident Baptist minister was Reverend Enoch Towner, 1825 to June 16, 1825.

Under the Church of England, Long and Brier Islands constituted the parish of Westport in 1925. A church was built on Brier Island on the last side street on the road to South Point. Dissenters soon attracted the congregation and the edifice was consequently sold to Wesleyans Methodists who held church there until 1894, having a resident minister, Reverent Edward R. Brunegate, 1884-1885. The church was eventually sold for a barn.The cemetery is well kept, and at the summit of Church Hill.

As the ground has been cleared off, the oldest, broken stones have been destroyed. At present, the oldest stone is that erected to Eathel Davis, 1801. The first settlers buried their dead on much lower ground, and afterwards, removed them to the hill because of the high tides. No date can be found as to when the removal took place.

The chief occupation of the men is fishing. They fish in the Passage and sometimes go out 25 miles in the Bay of Fundy. Larger ships take loads of fish, lobsters and scallops to the New England states. Lobster fishing is very profitable. The most of the fishermen have good motor boats. The telephone system was introduced through Digby Neck to Westport in 1888. The company is located on Brier Island.

At an early date, Brier Island was visited by fishermen, mostly from the New England states. In the spring of 1769, David Welch, a native of Maine, accompanied by his wife and children, set out on a voyage to the island and established a fishing post there. Robert Morrell, a former resident of Maine, but recently of Sissibo, Digby County, joined Welch.As the fish were very plentiful, these men remained on the island as pioneers. They fished for a living, owning their own ships. The fish were carried to the older colonies and exchanged for provisions.

The early settlers lived in log houses built near the shore and thoroughly covered with moss and seaweed. Small sections were cultivated with the fish refuse. Messrs. Hubbard and Tillis settled on the island in 1878 and the families of Samuel Buckman and Jacob Medlar arrived. These people were United Empire Loyalists. A grant of Brier Island, dated Nov. 10, 1784 and registered in Grant Book,Crown Land Office, Halifax on the 16th of the same month in that year was issued to the following: Thomas Huggeford, 400 acres; Roger Pye and William Mussel, 20 acres each; William Lallit, Jonas Aikins and four others were granted the remaining. These men were for the most part, residents of Digby town and sold their Brier Island claims to future settlers.

The earliest mention of the Township of Westport in County Archives appeared in the apportionment of County Tax of 260 pounds, six pence, by the Grand Jury at General Sessions in Dec., 1839. As the local officers for that portion of the County had previously been appointed for"Long and Brier Islands", the township was doubtlessly founded in that year, though no Act of Parliament for that purpose has been discovered.

One of the most interesting pioneer Loyalists to reach Brier Island was Christiana Margaret, wife of Eathel Davis. She was born in New York on December 22, 1764, and was the second daughter of Adam and Catherine Hubbard. On August 11, 1783, Christiana married Eathel Davis, a native of New Haven, Conn. Both Mr.Hubbard and Mr. Davis had served in the British Army. Mr. Hubbard held the position of sergeant and had been a prisoner for three years. When the United Empire Loyalists were leaving New York on transports furnished by sir Guy Carleton, the families of Hubbard and Davis took passage.. Their destination was Quebec.

Mr. Davis expected to take up lands in Quebec, having a claim for that purpose as they were leaving property at New York valued at 1400 pounds, York money. However, after being on the vessel for nearly six weeks, the vessel put in to Shelbourne, N.S. In an official account, Governor Parr speaks of the "Clinton and the great sufferings and hardships of its passengers during their sojourn on the wintry seas." They were mostly women and children.

In the same account mentioned before, Parr speaks of the problem of finding homes for the winter for these people, the greater part of them being practically destitute.The Davis family remained in Shelbourne for the winter. Adam Hubbard was drowned April 14, 1784, leaving his wife with five children. The Davis and Hubbard families left Shelbourne for Weymouth in July 1784 with a number of government vessels, under the command of Capt. Connell.

After remaining at Weymouth four years, they removed to Brier Island being the seventh family on the island. On Feb. 13, 1801, Eathel Davis fell from the mast of a vessel, breaking his leg. He lived but three months after the accident.He died May 15th. Mrs. Davis was left with nine children, two having died in infancy. Her mother now lived with her and they toiled together in bringing up the children and working the land. Part of their allotment had been cleared for a garden and fields for grass. The cows fed on the grass but as much of their land was not worth clearing, they acquired a flock of sheep to graze upon their stony land. Mrs. Davis and her mother were experts at the spinning wheel, knitting needles and loom. Whenever a person was sick or injured on the island, Mrs. Davis was at once sent for. She had great skill as a doctor and grew many herbs for her medicines.

In 1778, and the following two or three years, the families of Charles Richards, Christian Klingsoehr, Capt.Lultit, Elisha Payson, Mitchell Lincon, Jonathan Payson,Dennis Sullivan,George Lafoley, three brothers of the same name of Rice, William Bailey, Moses and Loce Denton settled in the middle of the island. William Bailey and his four sons and three daughters were Empire Loyalists and his son Daniel was an architect and builder. His own house, which still stands, shows his modern ideas about architecture. There are double doors between the sitting room and parlor and a curious winding stairway.

Squire Elisha Payson was one of the leading men of the island and was excise and tax collector. The first sailing vessel built on Brier Island was called "Heroine" and was constructed by Elisha Payson for West Indian trade, being a vessel of 120 tons capacity. People of note always stayed at the Squires when visiting the island. His youngest daughter, Mary, married Daniel Bailey.

The people failed ro procure deeds to their lands at that time, and were practically unknown and unprotected by the government. After a time however, all improved lands were secured to their owners by the King's Letter Patent. As Mrs. Davis did not have a deed to her land, some of her neighbors tried to encroach on her property. Failing to receive justice, she left her children in the care of her mother and walked all the 386 miles to Halifax and back. In Halifax, Mrs. Davis presented her case before the government and .received a deed to her land.. Mrs. Davis lived to be 93, dying on Feb. 14, 1858. At her death, Mrs. Davis had 44 grandchildren and a large number of great-grandchildren.

Some of Christiania's children went to Upper Canada, only Eathel Junior remaining on the island and a daughter, Mrs. Morrell. Descendents of Eathel are still living on some of the original Davis land but the Davis name has moved to other parts of Canada.

Aerial view of Westport taken in 1977 by the Canadian Forces from C.F.B. Shearwater. A helicopter from the base brought a load of used books for our library. They took this photo while making that trip.

43

A History of Northern Point Light

The first lighthouse at Northern Point Light was built in 1910. The first keeper was Charles Buckman, who was born and lived all his life at the north end of Brier Island. He tended the station for 40 years. During his stay there he was presented a l ong- service medal from King George VI. The oil lamp was first lit on Jan. 1, 1911. It had a red chimney and was a stationary beam.the bell erected as a Centennial Bell in front of the Digby Post Office was not the first bell used at Northern Point. It was the second bell that was on a cement block at the rear of the lighthouse and was rung by a protruding arm run from the shed and powered by a gasoline engine.the original bell ,made in 1882, was small in size and run by clockwork and weights. This bell was in use until 1968 as an auxiliary bell when power failed. It was run by a battery.

Harry McDormand lived at Northern Point in his earlier days. He said at the time there was a fair size settlement on the Point. Up until the fall of 1947, there was no road that cars could travel to Northern Point. There was only a cart track or a narrow path. In 1947, Terrance Robicheau with a team of oxen plowed the ground for the new road . He was helped by Harry Coggins and son, James.This new road was a much shorter way to Northern Point. In the summer of 1951, an artesian well was drilled on the hill opposite the house.In December, 1948, electricity was installed and a new fog alarm in the form of a horn was placed at Northern Point.

There have been a number of lightkeepers. After Charles Buckman died in March, 1940, his son, Franklin took over until December, 1941. At that time, Frederick Moore, a war veteran, became keeper.. He retired in December, 1957. Percy Welch, a veteran and former keeper at Peters Island Light took over until March, 1961 when Lemuel Greenwood took on the job. Wickerson Lent became keeper in 1978. The last keeper before the light was automated was Lawrence "Pete" Welch who had been a light keeper for Peters Island. The light was automated in 1983.

The old house at Northern Point was built a few years after the lighthouse and was there until May, 1968.,when the new house and lighthouse were completed, The present dwelling is a bungalow. The fog alarm and lighthouse are in a combined cement block structure. The light is still red but it is a flashing one instead of stationary.

Northern Point Light in the early 1900's. The official name for this Light is Grand Passage Light and Alarm Photo courtesy Mary Graham

Northern Point as seen in 1995

Paula Thompson married Stephen Newman in the Westport Church of Christ, September 14,1985. The couple live in Whale Cove and have two children.

Pond Cove in 1980. Three Westport children head for a cool swim. l. to r. are Charlotte and Susanna Norwood, centre is Cheryl Titus.

Westport Fire Chief Gordon Thompson accepts a cheque for $3000 from Marion Swift, president of the Westport Ladies Auxiliary. Mr. Thompson said the money was given to the Fire Department to purchase a 4-wheel drive auxiliary truck. Jan., 1981.

The home of Gary and Carolyn Frost located on Second Street and the corner of Canns Lane,1980.

47

The lobster canning factory which was located about where Dube Frost's shop is now. The factory was in operation during the early1900's. Note Peter's Island in background where there was also a lobster canning factory in years past.Photo courtesy Mary Graham

The Slocum Boot Shop building in Irishtown. This is the place where Joshua Slocum worked on leather boots when he was a young lad. It is now a registered Heritage Property.. (1990)

The house wasn't burning, only the grass in this March 11,1981 photo.
At left is Walt Titus. The house in the background was later torn down
to make way for the new house owned by Gordon and Marie Thompson.
The old house was known as the Coggins residence and Florence
Denton's childhood home.

It was bound to happen. The first tour bus arrived in Westport on
September, 1990. The bus brought a group of whale watchers.

Approaching Brier Island by Sea
From the <u>Nova Scotia Pilot, 1930.</u>

GRAND PASSAGE Grand Passage, between Brier and Long Islands, is narrow and contains several dangers, but the principal difficulty connected with its navigation is the great velocity of the tidal currents through the channel.

CHANNELS At the southern end of Grand Passage there is a channel on each side of Peter Island, that on its western side being the shoaler and narrower of the two, with a depth of 2-1/2 to 3-1/4 fathoms and clear of danger. The eastern channel has a depth of 6 fathoms.

NORTH POINT LIGHT, is shown from a white square wooden tower, 34 feet high, surmounted by an octagonal lantern painted red, located on North Point, the northeastern point of Brier Island, at the northern entrance of Grand Passage.

FOG SIGNAL A fog bell at the lighthouse is struck.

PETER ISLAND LIGHT is shown from a white octagonal tower, 44 feet high, surmounted by a red lantern, erected on Peter Island at the south entrance to Grand Passage.

BEACONS A reef extends north-northeastward from Peter Island to a distance of about 200 yards; the end of the reef is marked by a black iron spindle, surmounted by a spherical cage, 33 feet in height, which should be given a berth of not less than 50 yards when passing between it and Passage Shoal.An iron spindle surmounted by a slatwork drum, 10 feet above the water, the whole painted red, is erected on Bald Rock.

GRAND PASSAGE BELL BUOY A bell buoy, painted in black and white vertical stripes, marked "Grand Passage," is moored in 27 fathoms 1.1 mile 190 degrees from Peter Island Lighthouse.A red conical buoy marks the extremity of the shoal water off Dartmouth Point.

PASSAGE SHOAL with about 5 feet of water, shows a tide rip.; it lies in the middle of the passage, 346 degrees 800 yards from the lighthouse on Peter Island and 700 yards from its nearest shore.A can buoy, painted red and black with horizontal bands, is moored immediately northward of the shoalest rock of Passage Shoal.

COW LEDGE extends nearly 500 yards off the Long Island shore of the northern entrance of Grand Passage; its highest part uncovers soon after high water. A black conical buoy is moored 100 yards north-westward of Cow Ledge Shoal. A red spindle beacon, surmounted by a slat-work drum has been located on Cow Ledge.

COW LEDGE SHOAL with about 2-1/2 fathoms of water lies 500 yards northward of the highest part of Cow Ledge, and 600 yards 114 degrees from the northern point of Brier Island.

FREEPORT is on the eastern side of the passage and is entered by a narrow channel when the tide is rising. Passenger steamers call at Freeport from St. John and Yarmouth.

WESTPORT HARBOR, Brier Island is entered from Grand Passage. The harbor is open year round.

ANCHORAGE Close in on Brier Island there is good anchorage off the town of Westport in 5 to 7 fathoms mud bottom, with the Baptist Church bearing 256 degrees; only exposed to winds from the northeastward, and even then the water is always smooth at the anchorage recommended.

WHARVES There are several wharves in the harbor, but none of them extend below low-water mark. The Government pier affords good landing, with depth of 15 feet at low water. Westport carries on a considerable trade in fish, and from it limited supplies may be obtained. A small supply of fresh water may be procured from wells. Storm signals are shown at Westport.

PILOTS Pilots for St. John, New Brunswick can be obtained at Westport.

TIDES The mean high-water interval at Grand Passage is 10h. 37m.; mean range of tide 18.2 feet and spring range of tide 20.8 feet.

CURRENTS The current commences running to the southward fully half an hour before high water by the shore and runs with great velocity through Grand Passage, especially through the two channels at its southern entrance, where it attains a velocity of from 5 to 6 knots.

Directions - West of Peter Island - In making the southern entrance of Grand Passage steer for the bell buoy in the approach and pass on either side of it.

To pass westward of Peter Island keep in mid-channel, bearing in mind that the flood current sets with great strength directly on the southern point of Peter Island. When through the channel, if calling at Westport, steer to the northwestward for the anchorage described above.

Caution, however, is necessary in attempting the anchorage off

Westport without the assistance of local knowledge, as the tides in the entrance, with a velocity of 5 or 6 knots, form eddies and whirlpools likely to bring a vessel round against her helm and cause her to be stranded.

The holding ground off Westport is good, but the usual anchorage is too close inshore for large vessels; if farther out,vessels should moor, as the eddies would cause a single anchor to foul.

Life would be very dull without the mail. The Post Office is open six days a week but mail is only delivered Monday through Friday. The truck arrives on the 11 a.m. ferry, the mail is "put up" by noon usually and the truck leaves again for Digby on the 2 p.m. ferry. This is the routine in 1995.

When North Point, Brier Island bears 285 degrees, the vessel will be clear of Cow Ledge Shoal, and by keeping Peter Island lighthouse in sight, will pass a long way to the eastward of Northwest Ledge. After passing Cow Ledge Shoal, Long Island may be approached to the distance of 200 yards, but the northern point of Brier Island should not be rounded within 600 yards.

EAST OF PETER ISLAND On nearing the passage steer to pass between the whistle buoy and the buoy off Dartmouth Point, and pass-mid-channel eastward of Peter Island, and keep mid-channel to the northward until Peter Island Lighthouse bears 179 degrees, then proceed through the northern entrance with the marks already given.

If intending to anchor at Westport, after passing Peter Island, round the beacon on the shoal spit off the northern end of the island and pass between the beacon and Passage Shoal, on which the flood sets with great strength.The foregoing directions for entering Grand Passage from the southward are adapted for flood tide and a leading wind, and any departure therefrom must be contingent on the state of the tide and direction of wind.

Two of the older homes in Westport. House at left is owned by Huck and Caroline Norwood. At right,house is owned by Rikki Bolstad

*Fish plant workers had to cross the Passage in the fishing boat **Elaine P.**when the ferry was broken. (1980)*

Jason Graham and Annette Guier took part in a Westport Days parade.(1980)

Three enterprising Westport youths were out looking for empty beer bottles in December, 1980. Donnie Moore, r. said their cart should be pulled by a horse but they found it makes a perfect carrier for bottles. With Donnie are Derek Graham, l. and Darren Frost.

Sometimes strange things happen in Westport. One morning, people woke to find the outdoor toilet from Pond Cove had been placed in front of the Post Office.

Winter scene

You can also see "different" types of vehicles on the road. This was Ricky Buckman moving a piece of playground equipment.
Photo by Thomas E. Norwood

Glen Welch, l. and his brother, Bill hauling lobster traps aboard the **Corn Cob**, *winter, 1993 Photo by Dan Norwood*

The People.......

People gather on the Government Wharf to watch the Joshua Slocum Rowing Race, August, 1991. Photo by Thomas E. Norwood

Viola Garron at her 90th birthday party held in the Westport Recreation Hall. With her is Victoria Rose Mount, age 1 who came to help Viola celebrate. Victoria is the daughter of Sterling and Angela Mount.

It's All In The Cold Cream
Viola Garron Serenely Celebrates 90 Years
February 9, 1993

I think I've found the Fountain of Youth--in Westport! Now before you start to laugh, let me tell you about Viola Garron. She was 90 years old Feb. 6. She looks and acts more like someone 40 years younger. Her face has nary a wrinkle, skin as smooth as a baby's. I felt it, it's true. Viola laughs a lot, smiles even more and has a memory that compares favourably with the smartest computer. Ask her about a shipwreck in 1918 and she'll give you all the details.

The names of her gal pals from even earlier come easily to the tip of her tongue. There was Madeline, Vienna, Irene, Velma and Mary Lou. The girls used to hang around together, walking up one street and down the other when this Brier Island village was a much busier place and three-masted schooners stood at anchor in the harbour.

Viola says the reason she is healthy today is because she's always walked a lot all her life. Arthritis has slowed her a bit in that department but hasn't stopped her from picking cranberries and strawberries. She's never had an operation of any kind.Viola says she's been content with her life and never really had any bad times. "I've enjoyed my life, never had no real trouble outside of being poor but everybody was in them days," she smiles.

Rocky Start

Viola had a rocky start in life in more ways than one. Her parents lived beside the rocky shores of Northern Point, facing the boisterous Bay of Fundy. The village of Westport was a mile or more away by footpath. Her childhood ended abruptly when she was seven. Her father, George O'Connell died of pneumonia at age 71. This left her mother, Clara Stella (Buckman) with three young children and no income.

As Viola points out, there were no social programs available in those days to help a young widow. Her mother was forced to give up the family home. Young Viola was sent to live with her grandmother for a short time, then with her Aunt Katie and Uncle Charlie Buckman who kept the light at Northern Point.

Later she lived with other families on Brier Island, helping with

60

young children and doing housework while she attended school. She recalls boarding with one family for 25 cents a week.

"I remember when I was nine or 10, doing the ironing in one house. There was no ironing board, just a board over the table,"When Viola was 15, she went back to live at the lighthouse with her Aunt and Uncle. This time, she was paid $1.50 a week and was their maid. Her Aunt Katie was a dressmaker and frequently away for the day.In addition to household duties, Viola was called upon many times to take care of the light. "There was a good many times I had to tend the light. It was just a kerosene lamp with big thick glass   around the lamp. When my uncle went fishing, I used to go up and clean it for him and clean the windows."

Her face lights up as she recalls one day when she got stuck in the lighthouse. She says there was a trap door at the top of the stairs. When she got up by the light, she put the trap door down, then stepped on it. It got stuck! "I had to stay up there until Uncle Charlie came in from fishing. When he came around the point in his dory, I hollered to him and told him I was stuck. Grandma had called to me, wanting me to get Charlie's dinner. I told her I couldn't, I was stuck!"

In 1920, when she was 18, Viola married Leonard Garron. Lennie was 21 and a fisherman. The couple had known each other since grade school. Viola says Lennie lived in the first house she'd pass coming into the village from Northern Point. "I used to go by his house every day."

She says in the summer, she'd sometimes walk into the village several times a day. At that time, there were eight other houses she'd pass before reaching Lennie's place. All those houses are long gone, now only a memory to a very few. Viola says she is now the oldest person living in Westport.

She and Lennie had seven children, six of whom were born in the 175 year old house she lives in today. The couple moved to her present home in 1925. "My first child was born Feb. 19, 1921," Viola notes. Then she proudly names her sons and daughters: Alfred, the eldest, lives in St. John; Alva, Maureen, Iris, Beth, George and Eldridge live in Westport. Iris lives with her mother in the winter. The family now includes 12 grandchildren; 26 great-grandchildren and three-great-great-grandchildren.

Lennie died 25 years ago at age 67. For a time, her youngest son,

Eldridge lived with her after Lennie died. Viola says she has always stayed busy, either making quilts or knitting. Her family members visit every day. Viola has, of course, seen many, many changes on Brier Island. Westport once had a band and bandstand; a movie theatre; Temperance Hall; a population of over 600; regular freight and passenger service by steamboat; many more fishing boats in the harbour and ox teams on the dirt roads.

Now at the mention of ox teams, Viola starts to smile. She tells about the cow her father and Grampy John Thompson trained to haul wood. "My father used to yoke up the cow and hook it to a sled he made and they used that to haul out their wood. My father could do anything. He used to make wooden swivels for the lobster fishermen. He'd whittle them in the winter and sell them for a cent apiece. That's history."She also recalls the time the snowbanks were so high on the New Lane across from the Baptist Church that a man was able to drive his ox team under the snowbank. "It used to snow much more in years past than it does today," she adds.

Viola says she doesn't mind at all the way Westport has changed in recent years,with many tourists now visiting the island every summer. "It's always good here. It's good to see the people. It was nice in them days cause we didn't know any better. We had no ice, no electricity, no plastic bags, no TV. I don't know what in the Dickens we ever did without plastic bags and containers. We had no fridges, no nothing!

"We first had electricity in 1938. We had just one bare bulb hanging down. Before that, we used kerosene lamps."A trip to Digby was a rare event. "We used to go to Digby with Lloyd Blackford with the mail We washed clothes with a scrubboard and when they'd freeze outside in the winter, we had to bring them in and just hangthem wherever we could. You couldn't leave them out because there would be a gale of wind."

Members of Viola's family honoured her with a birthday dinner, Feb. 6, at the Westport Recreation/Fire Hall. She welcomed over 100 guests and cut three birthday cakes. One of the gifts she noted was a box containing 90 Super Bar (rip off) lottery tickets. Viola has always been an avid Bingo player and in recent years, she's enjoyed trying her luck with "scratch" tickets and the rip off lottery tickets. Though she says she had a lot of fun opening each ticket, she notes she only won $8 from the 90 tickets!

Viola says she's been quite content to live on Brier Island. She's visited Boston, St. John and Yarmouth but says Brier Island is the best place to be.She's looking forward to many more happy years and offers a bit of advice to those who wish to remain "wrinkle-free.""I always put Ponds Cold Cream on my face every night before I go to bed. And if I get in bed and forget it, I get right back out and put some on!

Viola Garron continues to live in her own home on Brier Island. She was recently honoured on her 92nd birthday with a party in her home.

A 1920 view of Western Light, officially known as Brier Island Light and Alarm . Photo couretsy Florence Denton

Bill Buckman, Fish Splitter
November 21, 1979

He sits beside the window wearing the cap, sweatshirt, jeans and black rubber boots that are his "uniform". He is knitting bait bags for lobster traps and glancing occasionally at the TV set on top of the refrigerator."That's our Christmas money," he says, indicating the pile of bags he's already made.

William Charles Buckman, age 44, professional fish splitter. He doesn't style himself as a professional though he admits he's been working at his trade since he was sixteen.Bill Buckman was born at Northern Point Lighthouse on Brier Island. He has spent his entire life on this four mile by one and one-half mile island, the most westerly bit of inhabited land in Nova Scotia. Bill's grandfather was keeper of the Northern Point Light for 40 years.

"Get the gold medal," he tells his son, Ricky. A faded, green satin case is brought out. Inside on the red velvet is a gold medal bearing the likeness of George V and Queen Mary. It was given to Grandfather William Charles Buckman in honour of his 40 years of service to his country.

Bill lived at Northern Point until he was eleven. Today a gravel road provides access to the Point. "It was only a wheelbarrow path when I was a boy," Bill recalls. "We had no electricity, no phone."

He has creased, tan and white snapshots showing himself and his sister, Mildred K. with their mother in front of the old lighthouse. It has been torn down and a modern tri-pod light signal gives notice of the rocky shore."The old bell from there is in front of the Digby Post Office now.They wanted a monument for the post office so Herbert Closson and I went up and got the bell and Herbert took it to Digby," he said.

Bill is the only survivor of his family. His mother, the former Mildred Pearl McDormand, died of leukemia when she was 43. His sister died of a stroke at age 31. His father, Franklin Charles, died three years ago.He is divorced from his first wife. His second wife, Margaret, came here from Culloden, a village near Digby. She brought her daughter, Melody. Bill had two sons, Charles, now 14, and David, 13. He and

Margaret have another son, Richard, called "Ricky", who is 12.Melody, now 15, is an honour student. This summer she went to Regina to visit her father whom she last saw when she was six. It was her first plane trip; first trip west.

Bill provides for his family by working at the D.B. Kenney fish plant most of the year. He stands on a wet, cement floor in the back of the plant, splitting fish eight hours a day, five, sometimes six days a week. He splits about 10,000 pounds of pollock, cod, and hake a day. He makes $5 an hour. Twice a day he takes a coffee break.

"Nobody's ever told me I could or couldn't have a coffee break. I just come home, morning and afternoon," he shrugs.

"There's no need for anyone to tell me what to do at work. You know what you're going to be doing all day, as long as the fish lasts, it's the same thing all the time," he continues.Everything he splits goes to be salted in the 40 large tanks which line the long walk from the front door to the back where Bill works.

At the fish plant, a fork lift whizzes busily back and forth in the crowded room. The fumes from the propane-fueled engine bother him."Gives me a headache and feels like my eyeballs are screwing right out of my head," he complains.

The cement floor bothers him, too. "Boy,that's hard on the feet."This brings Bill back to reminisce about the old days."When I started work, I made $12 a week, worked from seven in the morning until six at night, ten hours a day, six days a week.

"In those days, when you made $12 a week, you got it all. Today when you make $5 an hour, you don't get that. The government takes out a big whack."I went to work in the fish plant because that's all there was. It was either that or starve to death. I started work in that fish plant they tore down last winter, owned by Edgar McDormand."Off there at Edgar's in the cold of winter, we used to throw the fish guts on the floor and they'd freeze right there at your feet. I worked the year round then.

The floors used to be made of wood but they made them put in cement. Today everything is clean, stainless steel. Back then in the buildings, nothin' was ever scrubbed or cleaned. "They went around twice a year with a bucket of whitewash. I don't know if the fish tastes any different but it's clean.

65

"In the old days, you'd put dry fish in a box and if the top didn't go down far enough, you'd jump on it with both feet. Now they have hydraulic pressure."It was wicked in the old days, course there was more air to them old buildings, smell blew right out. We never noticed it but probably people coming in did.

"They salted fish then, salt came by boat from Turks Isle, West Indies. It was a lot coarser than this Nova Scotia salt that comes in plastic bags. Everything was boxed and shipped to the West Indies.

"We used to get paid last thing Saturday night. Now we're paid Thursday at noon. Used to get paid cash then.

"Today the building is heated. Years ago we used to have an old oil barrel which would heat a circle around it. They'd have a bucket of hot water sitting on top of it and when your fingers got frozen, you'd put them in it to thaw out. There was no such thing as insulated boots in those days.

"Another big change is the method of handling fish. We used to haul the fish from the boat off a ramp in a cart, 2,000 pounds at a time. We'd dump'em on the floor, pitch'em onto a scale, weigh'em, dump'em in a tank, pitch'em in a box, dress'em, put'em on the splittin' table, fire them into a tub to be washed, pitched into a cart and wheeled out to a tank for salting. Now we aren't allowed to pitch any fish. Everything's done with a fork lift."

Bill spends a lot of his spare time with his sons. He takes them with him nearly everywhere he goes. "That's the way it's always been," he said.He hopes they will continue in school. "I finished grade seven. Things is altogether different now. If a fellow got to grade six or seven then, he thought he knew it all. By the time he got older, he found he didn't know nothing."

Margaret, a deeply religious person, faithfully shepherds the children to Sunday School and church each week.Bill taught his boys how to use a chain saw this past winter. They cut firewood to fuel their three wood stoves. He also collects driftwood for fuel but notes, "It's hard on the stoves.

"We burn it in them things out there because they don't cost too much," he says, gesturing toward a sheet metal stove. "It would ruin that," he says, pointing to the new, white enamel wood cookstove.

The children also help their father gather "pennywinkles" in season, another way to earn a bit of extra money."I take them up Digby Neck to Centreville to sell, haven't got any idea where they sell them. They might steam them out and sell'em to the tavern," he suggests.Margaret comes in to add, "The kids love them, steam them out, put'em in butter," she smiles.

"She should have been up there at the camp Saturday night when that fellow was running around naked up there. I heard him say, 'well, I got all my clothes off, now I'm going in that trailer,'" Margaret continues. "I had the butcher knife ready for him."

The Buckman family owns a camper. They like to take the kids camping weekends at nearby campgrounds."Lately, we've been able to go camping and travel a little," Bill says, "I've got it in my head I'd like to have a canoe, but I'm scared to death of it." He knows how to row a boat but doesn't know how to swim.

"I don't think there's too many around here who does," he observes.Does he ever think of living anywhere other than Westport?

"Every day," he answers quickly. Then he reflects, "there ain't too much around to be choosy about now."

What is it he dislikes about this quiet fishing village?"Same as everybody else: ferries. Can't get away, can't get back."What about another job, a different type of work?"There's lots of things I'd like to try to do for a living. I think of something every once in awhile. You always think the grass is greener on the other side," he says quietly.

He's been with the Kenney firm for 13 years. It's the only fish plant on the island now. He puts into the Canada Pension Plan and can retire when he's 65. "But I've got a long way to go," he sighs.

He no longer works year round. "I could work the year round if I wanted to, everybody could but they just don't want to.

Last year, he quit work in February. "It took eight weeks to start getting my unemployment checks. These fishermen around here knock off work and start collecting their unemployment in two weeks."

Twenty-eight years of whacking fish apart and tearing out their back bones. Ten-thousand pounds of fish every day. And he has never cut himself. "

Bill Buckman working in his shop in Westport, making a bait bag.
Photo by Thomas E. Norwood (1989).

Ricky Buckman, 1986.Photo by Thomas E. Norwood

Bill and his sister, Kay Photos courtesy of Bill Buckman

David Buckman, May, 1987. Photo by Thomas E. Norwood

Bill splitting fish in 1984.

Bill Buckman and Walter Lent working at Neil Peter's fish plant.
Photo Thomas E. Norwood

Buckman Family on a fishing trip. Northern Point Light in
background.Photos: courtesy Bill Buckman

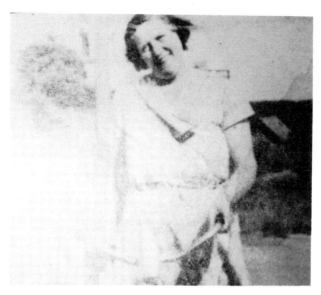

Mildred Buckman, Bill's mother

Bill and his sister, Kay Photos courtesy of Bill Buckman

The Irishtown wharf in 1980 before the rock break was built.

Wickerson Lent Retires to the Mainland
"The wind blowing through the poplars sounds almost the same."
May 23, 1984

Wickerson Lent was sitting on the well cover outside his South Range home on the Sissiboo Road, enjoying the spring sunshine.A native of Brier Island and a lighthouse keeper for 24 years, Wick has retired to the country."You can't hear the waves crashing on the shore, don't you miss it?" I asked.

Wick looked around the land and replied thoughtfully, "Well, you can hear the wind blowing through those poplar trees and it sounds almost the same."And if we really get homesick for Brier Island, we can go over and sit on those rocks beside the garden. We brought them when we moved, used them to hold down the tarp," he laughed.

Wick and his wife, Emily, are slowly unpacking their possessions which they brought in April from the lightkeeper's house at Grand Passage Light, Brier Island.He had been keeper there since 1978. Prior to that, he served as assistant keeper at Brier Island Light on the western tip of the Island. This light was originally built in 1809 and its beam can be seen up to 17 miles at sea.

Wick began working at that historic light in April, 1961. "My first job as a lighthouse keeper was filling in for the keeper at Grand Passage Light. That was in 1960. The keeper at that time was Percy Welch. Percy moved to Brier Island light."Wick said he decided to take the lighthouse job because fishing was becoming increasingly difficult for him."I'd been a fisherman all my life but it was getting a little bit too tough. With an artificial leg, it was just too much."He lost his right leg in a hunting accident when he was 16 years old.

He moved to Brier Island Light with his first wife, the late Madeline Doty, and their four children.At that time, there was no electricity at that part of the Island. "We had no refrigeration and used kerosene lamps for lighting we did have a phone, however."

He and two other men kept a 24-hour watch. The light then was a kerosene vapour lamp which had to be lit each evening and extinguished every morning. The fog alarm was a type B diaphragm which the keepers had to start every time the fog rolled in.We got electricity in the houses shortly after we moved to the duplex.

74

"We were there quite awhile before the light changed over to electric. There was an old house across the road from the duplex that's there now." Wick recalled there was one small source of electricity on the island and that was in the fog alarm buildings.

"We had a motor turning in reverse that generated enough power for that building. The men on the station would take their electric razors to the fog alarm building," he laughed.He said his pay in those early years was $2,180 per year. He worked with Percy Welch, keeper and George Denton, assistant keeper. The number of keepers at Brier Island Light now has been reduced to one.

Though Wick foresees the day when most lighthouses will be automatic, he doesn't think it's a good idea."I know from experience when I was fishing in thick fog, it's a good thing to know that there is someone around there. I know they have radar and things now, but those machines are only as good as the man who made them." He said he has never regretted his decision to become a lighthouse keeper.It was a solitary life but he has always enjoyed quiet and said he was never bored. For nearly 20 years, he kept a daily record of weather and current events.

The job also gave him a chance to pursue a lifelong interest in birds."I've always been interested in birds, ever since I was a little fellow. When ever I'd see a strange bird, I would run to Mrs. Ann Bailey. She had a book on birds and would help me find information."He has seen 390 different species of birds so far, all but two of those on Brier Island.

"The only two I've seen off the island are the piliated woodpecker and the great horned owl," he added.Wick became an authority on birds and many bird watchers would visit the Brier Island light station to talk to him. He became friends with many well-known authorities on birds such as the late Robie Tufts, Cyril Coldwell, Dr. Harrison Lewis and Willet Mills.Mr. Mills worked with Wick banding birds for many years.In addition to bird watchers, many people interested in wildflowers came to the western tip of the Island.

Wick said he enjoyed talking with the tourists. So why did he move to South Range?"I love the country and the quiet and we are rid of ferries," he laughed."I wouldn't have minded retiring on the Island but it's so hard to get to and from the place."He hopes now to have time to visit his children. A son, Chester, lives in Kentville. Capt. Harry Lent is in Hubbards. Son Brian lives in Pickering, Ontario and daughter, Faye is in Toronto.

He also enjoys hunting and gardening. Wick brought about 400 houseplants with him from Brier Island including many African violets."All I have left in Brier Island now is a cemetery lot. I haven't even got any relatives left on the Island.He does have memories and those 20 years of journals to remind him of the days spent beside the sea.

Wickerson Lent ,1994. Photo taken on the Westport ferry slip.

Jim Maclauchlan's Story About The
Royal Canadian Dragoons
Told to the author in 1994

In April, 1993, Jim Maclauchlan told me about the time he was in the Royal Canadian Dragoons in St. John's, Quebec. He said he joined the Squadron in January, 1939. "The barracks were outside the city on the site of an old fort. There was a row of brick married quarters leading up to the guard house. Inside was the barrack's square, surrounded by barrack blocks of the RCD and the Royal Canadian Regiment (the infantry); the officer's quarters and a building containing the men's messes. There were classrooms, offices and a ballroom as well as the quartermaster's office; stores; kitchens and mess hall; tailor, barber and cobbler.

"Behind all that was the Vet hospital and saddler and farrier. Past that was the hospital, garage and stables. There was a riding school and sports field. Old ramparts partly surrounded the complex. We had big draft horses that we used to use to carry rations to the married quarters once a week."

Jim said there were seven men in his recruit class. "We were issued winter and summer uniforms, boots which had to be dyed and polished to a high gloss, sword, rifle, whip, grooming kit and British warm,a short coat for riding as well as fatigue (work) clothes. We wore riding breeches and puttees, all World War I issue. Oh yes, and muskrat fur hats in the winter. It used to get down to 18 below zero F. there."

Jim said he lived in a large barracks room with all his kit on pegs and a shelf behind each bed. "Each Friday night, the floor was scrubbed by hand and even the buckets were shined Saturday morning, everything, including horses and saddles were made ready for inspection. Bedding was rolled a certain way. Steel helmet went on top. On the bed, sword, scabbard, rifle with bolts and magazine out was laid out in order. Everything was oiled and shined to perfection for the inspection by the commanding officer."

"We recruits went through the usual training," Jim continued. He said this included sword and whip drills. They were given a scarlet covered book emblazoned with the Regimental Badge, giving the history of the RCD. "We were not allowed out the gate until we smartened up and not then without the approval of the Old Soldiers. There was no slouching down town.

"Soon after I joined, we paraded to the Anglican Church. There was a light rain and we wore fur hats, cloaks and swords which clattered during the seating. Soon the steam rose from the damp cloaks and the church smelled like a stable. People moved away from us. I recall a Lance Corporal chided me for putting a nickel in the collection plate. We were paid $1.10 a day."

Jim said on a typical day, trumpet sounded reveille at about 6. "We dressed in minutes and rushed over to the mess hall for cocoa. Then we went to the stables. We cleaned out the stalls (recruits couldn't use forks) and gave the horses a feed of hay. Those who were riding, saddled one horse and got another ready to lead. Then we headed outside and lined up by 6:30 and rode about the surrounding countryside until 8 a.m. The horses were then watered and returned to the stalls. We were marched to breakfast. Then it was morning stables.

"Stalls were swept, horses groomed and saddles cleaned and polished. The stable was in the form of a 'K' with a feed room and operating table; a rotunda with water trough and four rows of stalls. There was one for the officer's chargers and draft horses and one for each troop. One morning soon after joining, the troop sergeant told me that the Sergeant Major wanted to see my horse. The Sgt.Major was Tommy Sheehy, a short-tempered, red-faced Irishman. I led the horse out and Sheehy put his hand over his eyes and yelled, 'Get that f—king thing out of here.'

"I remember one guy who was really lazy. He would only groom one side of his horse, the side they could see. He eventually got caught. Later the horses were watered and inspected, then fed their ration of oats. Each man held two feed tins and the horses knew what was coming. The trumpet sounded and the horses were fed. We then line up for the Sgt. Major's usual blast and marched to dinner.

"The afternoon program consisted of lectures and drill. Then it was the evening stables. In the straw sheds, there was a pile of steaming wet straw which was mixed with fresh straw. We carried it into the stall by the armload. Blankets were put on the horses and so ended the day."

Jim said there was a stable picket all night and twice a week a hot feed was prepared for the horses. Those on picket duty stayed in the guard houses and took turns at the stables.

On Wednesday afternoons, the recruits were free to do whatever they wanted. "Black Hose brewers put on a barrel of beer for us. Every two weeks, an all ranks 'smoker' was held in the men's mess. It was an evening of beer, stories and song. Once a month we held a regimental dance. We wore scarlet tunics and blue trousers with a yellow stripe. A busload of girls in evening dress came from Montreal."

Jim said discipline was very strict at the base. "I got seven days CB (confined to barracks) because my horse's hoof scraped the fetlock of the one ahead. I could have had my horse cut to pieces. You were either on parade or off parade. If you were off parade, the NCO who barked at you all day would say, "Have a beer, Mac.' The line was clearly drawn."

He recalled the formal dress worn for formal parades: a brass helmet with horsehair plume; scarlet tunic with white cross belts; white gauntlets; blue pants with gold stripe. The horses wore gold decorated horse blankets and a white head rope.

Jim said the riding school was a large shed with a tanbark floor, This was where the recruits were taught horsemanship and practiced for musical rides. "We had an English corporal called Sid Quartley. We had to cross our stirrups, even when we jumped. One day when we got missed up he came out with this: 'When I was a little boy, my mother gave me a box of tin soldiers. One day I lost them, but now I've found them.' Or he would say, 'It's men like you that make men like me **Hate Bloody Men Like You!**'

"One day each spring, we had a mounted sports day. There was jumping, tent pegging (you galloped with a drawn sword and picked up a peg stuck in the ground). We also did that with lances. In the summer, there were maneuvers and long marches. Full marching order was steel helmet, bandoleer, rifle in a leather bucket on the right side and sword on the left. We carried a feed of hay and oats and spare horse shoes.

"An advance party went ahead and a field kitchen. They set up horse lines for the overnight stop. For lunch, we didn't stop but were handed a cup of tea and a sandwich. We ate the sandwich, drank the tea and kept going. We usually stopped by a lake so we could give the horses and ourselves a swim. The horses always came first. We slept by the horses and the officers were the last to turn in.

"With the outbreak of war, all that changed. We were given the option of signing on for active service. To their surprise, many did not. We were told we were going to the Middle East to patrol pipelines, along with many other 'buzzes'. The horses were left to be sold or destroyed, even Teddy and Gray who joined the Regiment in Belgium in the First World War. We didn't seem to be going anywhere. We were classed as armoured car in the tank division. Many recruits transferred to other regiments or arms of the Service. I wound up as a Stoker in the Navy."

Jim said he stayed in the horse regiment until the winter of 1941. In 1942, he joined the Navy and was supposed to go overseas three times but never went. "I got all ready to go and didn't. The war would be over before we had a chance." He stayed in the Navy until the end of the war. "I was out for two years, then joined the Air Force." He retired after 27 years in the military.

Jim said his years with the Royal Canadian Dragoons stayed with him. He has been to two reunions. Jim lives in Westport with his wife, Grace and their daughter, Janet. Until recent years, Jim was a familiar sight in the summer in Westport harbour, sailing in his 18 ft. Drascombe Lugger with red sails. He named his boat **Finest Kind.**

Jim MacLauchlan sitting on lobster traps in front of his Water Street home, 1994, before the new ferry wharf was built.

Bob MacDormand became the second pilot to land a plane on Brier Island with a passenger when he brought this Cessna down on Pond Cove on Feb. 15. 1995. He was accompanied by Arden Derby, who took this photo. Bob made a previous landing on Pond Cove in 1994. He says the first passenger flight to Brier Island was made in 1934 when a biplane landed in the field on the New Lane, touching down just after the cemetery and coming to a halt at a three-strand fence just below the present Bill Buckman residence. That plane was from the Malagash Salt Company. The two aboard got some boat gas and managed to take off and get back to Yarmouth without mishap. Bob was seven when this plane landed. He remembers Allison Denton picking him up so he could see in the cockpit.

Enjoying the music and the fun at a dance in the Fire Hall, l. to r. are Arden Derby, Dan Norwood, Vance Dixon, Gordon Thompson and Terry Albright.Photo by Thomas E. Norwood

Lawrence Gower and his dog, Pepper, out for a walk on the Gull Rock Road, 1993. Lawrence fished with George Clements for many years and later worked 10 years at the D.B. Kenney fish plant. He was 74 years old when this photo was taken. He lives in Irishtown.

Huck Norwood, standing and Lester Pugh stopped for a conversation on the Western Light Road, winter of 1991.

Corinne Titus, l. and Susanna Norwood at one of the Fire Department's Pancake Breakfast held on Saturday mornings in the Westport Community Hall. Photo taken in the fall, 1994.

Lois Pugh Lives In Former School
August, 1994

Lois Pugh ,80,lives in what was once Westport's first school. She said the home she shares with husband, Lester, is one of the oldest dwellings on the Island. "There's not a nail in it as far as construction goes."

Lois knows a great deal about the history of Brier Island. Her great-great-grandmother was Emma Potter from Bear River. Thomas Pugh was her maternal great-grandfather. "They bought this house. There is a beam in the attic with their daughter's name carved in it, Alice Pugh. She was my grandmother.

"It was at first just one room. Someone added the second floor along the way. I remember seeing the copper ceiling here when I was young. It was sky blue with gold leaf. I've been told this was a one-room school, one of the Dame Schools."

Lois lives on Church Street now but said when her house was built, Church Street didn't exist. "The road went to the eastward between Floyd Graham's and Don Glavins. There was also a house in-between there. This was just a cattle path. this was all farm land," she continued.

Lois said there was a house on the left at the end of Church street where her family lived when she was young. "We were all born there. My mother was Cynthia Cann. Her father and his brother were drowned off Northern Point in a overloaded fishing boat. They were George and Albert Cann. Cynthia was only a year old and her sister not yet born when this happened.

She said her grandparents, Albert and Alice (Pugh) Cann lived in the house which is now gone but was located by the present home of Don Glavin.Alice married again and lived in St. John.

Lois said her father was Boyd Graham. He married Cynthia, . They had seven children:Jean, Lois, Albert, Robert, Evelyn, Louise and Philip. Boyd was a fisherman who lived to be 84.

His fish shop was in front of the family home which was at the end of the present Church Street. Both the house and shop are now gone. Next to his shop was another belonging to Audbur Welch.

"People used to swim between those shops and around them and under them! It was a white sand beach. I think the wharves kept the sand in. There used to be two weirs up there too. They used to catch tuna in them. They'd bring them ashore and cut them up, everybody had a share."

Lois said a lot more people went swimming in the harbour when she was young. "People used to sit on the breastwork around the harbour, which at that time was all made of wood. They'd sit there with their sunshades and this was one of the best places to swim. We never could go down to Gull Rock way because of the tide. The water would be so warm here."

Lois said where there is a culvert under the road at the corner, there was in the past a "real bridge." It had rails and planks on the deck. "I remember a crowd of us standing on the bridge watching the eclipse of the sun. There was much more water up there at that time. There used to be as sluice gate. They used to flood it and cut the ice. I remember when the ice house burned.

"Now that's a mystery. Children used to go in there. It had big beams and we used to swing out the door of the ice house. No one ever knew how it burned, same as Mr. Morrell's barn. The ice house had electricity in it. It was operated by a Bowers. The shop the Graham's own now was a Rapole shop in years past."

When Lois mentioned the Morrell barn burning, she recalled George Morrell turned the former Methodist church at the head of the present Church street into a barn. "I remember seeing it burn. There used to be hundreds of barn swallows nesting in it. The spring after it burned, they all came back and kept circling round and round for days and making a terrible noise. I felt terrible. A few came back in later years."

Lois said there used to be a lobster canning factory in front of where Dougie Delaney lives now. "I can just remember them being there. We used to go down on the beach and see the shells going down there. There's nothing around now. This place was booming place at one time.

"There was a blacksmith shop. It was located where Lawrence Gower lives now, right in front of that house. Pete Dakin made anchors, horseshoes. He would have been Tony Dakin's great-great-grandfather.

"There was an ice cream parlor in a house next to where Danny Kenney lives now. It was called The Black Cat. It had little tables with two chairs and a counter. They made the ice cream themselves. They had fancy glasses and long spoons, special dishes for banana splits.

"Lester's father also had an ice cream parlor. For quite a few years.Out over the water. You went up steps to get up there. It was nice. They didn't have the liquor around then."

Lois said she enjoys walking and picking berries. "If you sit around, you've had it." She attended school here, and got a temporary school teaching license. Later she got a job as a waitress at The Pines Resort in Digby.

"I made more money there in four months than I did teaching school for a whole year. So I came home, helped my mother and went back to the Pines, later worked at the Grand Hotel in Yarmouth, then I married Lester Pugh."

Lois said she had known Lester all her life before their marriage. "We grew up together." They have been married 55 years and lived in their present home during that time.

"This was always home, it was my grandmother's home. I remember coming here when I was two years old. Mother and father lived here, all the brothers and sisters. Three generations have lived here."

Lois said her mother, Cynthia was a pianist for the silent movies. "She was a beautiful pianist. We always had a piano and organ in our home. We used to have duets. My mother sang alto, I sang soprano."

Lois said there is a record called The Old Village Choir which sounds like her mother and her singing. She said movies were first held in the Oddfellow's Hall. Later Gerald Strickland built a movie hall. The Temperance Hall was in back of the Baptist Church .

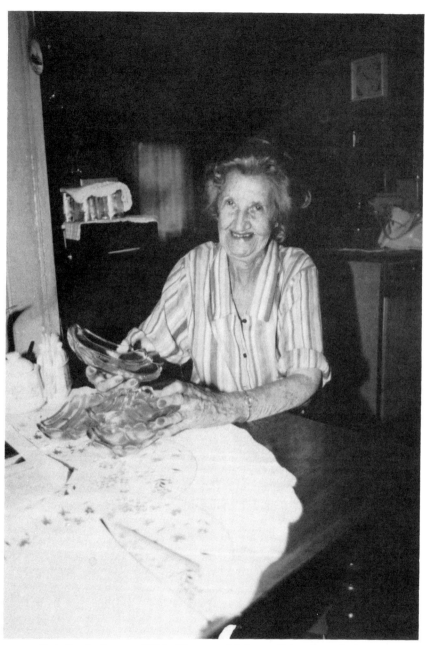

Lois Pugh, August, 1994, 80 years old, shows dishes from the ice cream parlour which was once in Westport. Lois is married to Lester. They live on Church Street in one of the oldest houses in the village.

At a Fireman's Pancake Breakfast in the Community Hall.
1994. l.to r. Amy Barnaby, Janie Derby, Mickie Barnaby and
Colin Derby. Standing in back is Clyde Stark, seated Roger Clements.

Children playing (1979) L. to r. Daniel Kenney, Sherri Titus, Annette
Guier, Susanna Norwood. Standing, Caroline Norwood. Background
is Myrna Garron's house (centre).

Roy Graham   Troy Frost

Jonathon and his mother, Wanda Graham pay for purchases. Joyce and Wally DeVries behind the counter.

Susanna Norwood and Brandee Welch

Phil Shea   *Janet Bailey*

91

Arden Derby telling a joke maybe? Arden owns the ambulance company which serves Long and Brier Islands. He lives in Westport with his wife, Jane and two children.

Glenda Welch and Crystal Ameriaut select a movie

Melinda Gaudet

Dot and Dolan Garron
Look Back Over 50 Years
August 1, 1987

Dot and Dolan Garron of Westport celebrated their 50th wedding anniversary on July 14. Dolan summed up the 50 years by saying, "We've had an interesting life and a darn hard life."The couple has known each other since early childhood. Adelia "Dot" Welch grew up at the lightstation on the western tip of Brier Island. Her half-brother, Albert Welch was the lightkeeper there.

Dolan, the son of Austin and Edith Garron, lived in the Village where his father was a fisherman. Dot went to Yarmouth School of Nursing and graduated in 1933. By that time, Dolan had experienced the tragic deaths of both his mother and father. His mother died at age 38 after a period of ill health. His father died a few years later at age 45, in a drowning accident in Grand Passage.

Shortly after his father's death, the couple were married in the Church of Christ parsonage in Westport.They spent their "honeymoon" in a farmhouse on the High Knoll on Brier Island at the home of Dolan's grandmother, Sara Jane Denton.

"We had $15 when we got married. That was quite a sum of money," Dolan smiled.After that first winter, they moved into their own home. Dolan worked at fishing and farming. "I did everything I could to make a dollar. I worked in Melbourne McDormand's fish plant, kept cows, hogs, raised a garden and a family."

The couple had four children and had Dolan's grandmother living with them when they made a decision that drastically changed their life. The year was 1953. They decided to move to the United States.

"We were having it rough. We had an opportunity and thought we would better the children by moving to the States," Dot began.They left their home, took only a few belongings and headed for Sullivan, Illinois. One son, Myron, age 17, chose to stay behind. He had a job working at the Bank of Nova Scotia in Freeport.

Dolan was 39 years old. He had always attended church but an event occurred while he was in his late 30's that made him want to know more about the different religions. He enrolled in Eureka College in Illinois where he studied for two years and was ordained a minister in the Church of Christ.

93

Dot noted they had $81 when they arrived in the States. She said she had mixed feelings about leaving Westport at that time."We thought the children might get a better education and I knew I could get work and make better pay," she explained.

Dot had a nursing job within two weeks of their arrival. They lived in a parsonage and "everything clicked along pretty good," Dolan continued. He preached in churches in the States for 10 years. When he had a period of poor health, the couple moved to Tennessee to be near their daughter, Brenda and family.

"There was no Christian Church there so I went to work as an inspector in a factory making engine parts," Dolan said.Dot continued to work, mainly as a maternity nurse. She retired when she was 62 years old.

In 1976, they decided to move back to Westport." Our eldest son, Myron talked us into it," Dot said, "adding they purchased their present home in 1977 and "had to start all over again setting up housekeeping."

They found many changes when they moved back to Westport."Westport is washing away rapidly," Dolan observed. He said he's seen the High Knoll area erode away at least 60 feet and land near Southern Point has washed away about 30 feet.

Dolan said a road used to go along the shore in the High Knoll area where now there are only boulders and the tide washes to the base of massive cliff."That area was known as the Hot Rocks when I was a kid. A lot of couples used to walk up there," he laughed.

In another area of the village where there is now only a rocky shore, Dolan recalled a large fresh-water pond where people used to swim."It was called the Dyke Pond and there was a great patch of sand in front of it. That pond never went dry," he added.He said fishermen used to dry their fish on the dyke wall. "That is all gone now, eroded away."

On July 14, Dot and Dolan had time to share memories with more than 100 relatives and friends who attended their anniversary party. It was held at the Westport Recreation Hall and began with an Anniversary Dinner served to 80 guests. The celebration continued with an Open House from 8 p.m. until midnight. The affair was arranged by their son, Myron.

The Garrons had 20 members of their immediate family staying with them in their home, including their only great-grandchild, Tisha Marie, age 13 months from Manhatten, Kansas.The three children who went with them to Illinois in 1953 now live in the United States. Daughter Edith lives in Kansas; Donald is in Mobile, Alabama and daughter, Brenda lives in New York State. Myron, who stayed behind to work in the bank, is a resident of Unionville, Ontario.

Dolan Garron died Oct. 29, 1987 at age 72. Dot lives in her own home in Westport.

Clyde Titus, lobster fisherman from Westport, points to the place on the side of his boat which was badly chaffed when the boat got caught under a piece of wharf and sunk early Saturday morning. Mr. Titus was unable to get the gasoline engine operating in time for the opening day of lobstering. (Nov. 26, 1980)

Terry Saunders
Reaching Out to Others Really Helps
December 21, 1983

Terry Saunders, a 40-year-old Westport resident, is severely handicapped due to a genetic disorder known as osteogenesis imperfecta.Osteogenesis Imperfecta is a Latin term meaning imperfect formation of bones. OI concerns a whole group of heritable disorders of connective tissues (bones, sclerae, skin and tendons) resulting in increased liability to fractures. It is also sometimes called Brittle Bone Disease.Terry says he believes most people with OI "are reasonably happy.""It's not an easy life in many ways but it's certainly not the worst thing that could happen," he smiled.

Terry is a co-founder of the Canadian Osteogenesis Imperfecta Society. He and Ontario resident, Joan Winterbottom, R.N. began planning the Society in 1980-81.He is vice-president of this Society. "They thought that was an ideal job for me," Terry laughed."I just dabble in everybody's business. But of course, if something happens to the president, I have to take over, so I am praying daily for her welfare. Our primary goal is to support the OI people and their families through counselling parents, especially when their children are very young," Terry explained.

"It's quite a traumatic thing for parents to suddenly realize they have an OI child," he added.Terry said another goal of the Society is to educate doctors about OI. "Many doctors don't know too much about it because it is not written up very well in their medical textbooks," he commented.

OI has been recognized in medical literature since 1788. There is evidence that it existed in 1,000 B.C. and was almost certainly the medical condition suffered by Ivar the Boneless in the 9th Century, A.D. Terry said the disorder is not racially determined nor limited to certain areas of the world.

"Osteoporosis, which is another bone disorder which results in easily breakable bones, is more or less confined to people in the northern hemisphere," he observed.He said there are many variations of OI. "I have one of the severe handicap cases. Some people, you wouldn't really know they had anything wrong with them," he added.Terry has never met another person with OI until the summer of 1982. He travelled by plane to Scotland to attend the Second International Meeting of the Brittle Bone Society.

"That is the name of the OI Society in Great Britain," Terry explained.He was there for eight days and had a chance to meet with more than 100 people with OI."I saw the many different levels of OI. I saw what was happening over there. Every Society spoke about what they were doing. You got a very good idea of what was happening around the world," he noted.

Terry said Mrs. Winterbottom also attended this meeting."We realized we had to do something when we got back," he said.They received a great deal of help and support from the American organization, Osteonesis Imperfecta Foundation,Inc. which was formed in 1970."We now have 50 paid-up members but we have contact with more than 150 families with OI. That would include an indefinite number of children with OI because some families have more than one member with the disorder," he stated.

Terry uses an electric typewriter donated by Citadel Office Supply, Yarmouth. He keeps in personal contact with many people with OI, especially in Atlantic Canada."I try to make sure the people here in this region are kept up to date," he said.

Another project is to secure government grants to get materiel printed and pay for office supplies. "This is one of the things I am working on personally to get the rest of the Society to agree with me that this is the way we go," he commented.He said most of the research on OI has been done in the United States and Great Britain."They have not yet been able to identify the exact genetic cause of OI. I don't know if I am exactly in favour of research which would lead to identifying the disorder in the womb," Terry said thoughtfully.I am not in favour of abortion. Abortion just turns me off," he added.

He said it would be good if doctors could advise prospective parents that they are likely to have an OI child. "I am in favour of that. Of course, we are also hoping scientists will be able to do genetic engineering to reprogram the gene that is giving the wrong instructions. Now the gene is not programmed to produce the proper collagen cells." Terry believes the Society will become more active in the future. He has made personal appearances on CBC-TV to discuss the disorder and the Society.

"I feel it is important for families with young children who have OI to know there is someone else out there with it too, someone they can contact, who understands what they are talking about," Terry observed.He said an Atlantic Chapter of the Canadian OI Society has recently been formed. He is corresponding secretary of this group.

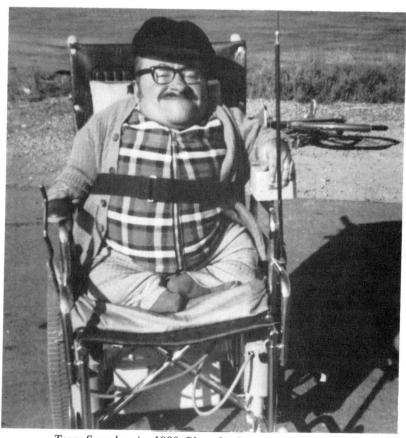

Terry Saunders in 1980. Photo by Grace MacLauchlan

Gertrude Welch Says ...
Westport's Not Like It Used To Be
August, 1994

Gertrude Welch lives in the same house she came to as a bride 66 years ago at age 19. Her husband,Lawrence died in 1969 at age 75. She and Lawrence had six children. All but one live on Brier Island. She says her many family members keep life interesting . She never lacks visitors and is always up on the latest news about the Village.

"My children drop in to visit me every day.. There's never a day goes by that some of them or all of them show up. I'm not afraid to live alone but I'll tell you, it isn't like it used to be around here. There seems to be a lot of strangers. "

But Gertrude says Westport just isn't the way it used to be in many ways. "It was a quiet life when I was growing up. We got our food by boat. Molasses came in great big kegs, same with vinegar and all that stuff,flour, everything like that came on the steamships from Yarmouth or St. John.

"A lot of people did their gardening in them days. What didn't went to Meteghan with their slack fish and traded them for vegetables.

"You didn't hear much about divorce. People stayed together whether they liked it or not! We never had electricity or paved roads, none of that stuff. People was more friendly. They visited each other more." Gertraude said for entertainment, they had a record player with cylinder records.

Gertrude was born in Freeport, Aug. 27, 1909, the daughter of Cora and Ervin Thompson. When she was just an infant, the family moved to Westport. Her father went fishing. Her mother was a midwife. Gertrude attended school in the old two-storey school still standing on the back road. (Second Street).

Her parents went to Boston when she was 16 and she attended school there for a year. They returned to Nova Scotia and her father went back to fishing.

"My mother was a midwife all her life. She learned this skill by working with Dr. Bishop in Freeport when she was just a young girl. I think she was about 15 or even younger shen she started helping him."

Gertrude said she went back to the states for awhile and lived with her aunts, Edith and Gertrude in Boston but she didn't like it there. "That was my third time there. I didn't want to go back again." So she married Lawrence whom she had known all her life. He too was a fisherman.

Their children are Connie (Bisson); Lorraine (Bezant) Lawrence "Pete"; Glenn; Bill and Philip. Philip lives in Cape Breton. Gertrude said all her children were born in her present home except Bill, the oldest. He was born in Boston. where she and Lawrence were living at the time.

Gertrude has traveled to every province in Canada and to many area s of the United States. "When I was a kid,I always wanted to go to Hawaii and the Rockies. When I got to the Rockies, I was quite satisfied to see Lake Louise and the Rocky Mountains. I walked in there and picked up a rock and was going to take it home but I forgot it.
Philip was there at that time, taking a special course. She never got to Hawaii but said now she has no desire to go.

"When I look back over my life, I am happy that I stayed in Westport. I don't want to live anywhere else. I tried it but I didn't like it."

Gertrude Welch in her home in Irishtown, 1994, age 84

Cora Thompson
"Nanny Cookie" Celebrates 90th
October 15, 1980

Cora Thompson, known to young and old alike as "Nanny Cookie," grandmother to nine, great-grandmother to 26 and great-great-grandmother to 11, celebrated her 90th birthday here Saturday. The occasion was marked by an Open House in the afternoon for her many friends and a family dinner in the evening for the more than 80 immediate family members. Mrs. Thompson received a money tree, numerous gifts and cards and the well-wishes of all who attended the event.

Though her life has spanned nearly four generations, Mrs. Thompson maintains good health and a lively interest in her ever-growing family. She clearly recalls events frrom her childhood and has kept scrapbooks for many years which detail past events of both Westport and neighboring Freeport.

Mrs. Thompson was born in Freeport, Oct. 13, 1890, the daughter of Benjamin and Rachel (Tidd) Prime. She grew up on a farm with five brothers and five sisters. She and an older sister, Janet Dillon, 96, of California, are the only surviving members of that family.Her girlhood days were always busy.

"We were a big family and we had to go to work at an early age," she recalled. Her jobs were usually doing housework but she also helped her mother card, spin and knit wool. "My sisters and I would knit those big fishermen's mittens and heavy socks. We sold them for 25 cents a pair. Any money we made we could keep. That's how we bought our clothes," she added.

Cora married Ervin Thompson of Westport when she was 18 years old. Mr. Thompson died 12 years ago. The couple had three children. Daughters Gertrude Welch and Verna Williamson live near their mother in Westport. A son died in infancy.She accompanied him to births and stayed on to help   the new mother and her family. When she came to live in Westport, she continued acting as midwife. She says today she has probably assisted at the birth of more than 100 babies."I have seen people born. I have seen them die. I have laid them out, gotten them ready to put in the casket," Mrs. Thompson said quietly. Her daughters added that their mother would not only act as midwife, she would move right in to help the family, doing the cooking, washing and cleaning. She also took care of older people for many years and acted as the island undertaker.

Mrs. Thompson said she has always worked hard all her life and has always gotten along well with everyone. She remains a friend to all who know her, especially the young people who never fail to wave when they pass by her house. They know usually "Nanny Cookie" will be there looking out over the harbour from the house which has been her home for the past 58 years. And she always waves back.

Cora Thompson with her daughters, l. to r. Verna Williamson and Gertrude Welch 1980.

Susie Glavin at her 94th birthday party, September, 1994

Susie Glavin
Islander Honored on Birthday
September 10, 1994

Everybody likes a birthday party but it's extra-special when the guest of honor is 94. Susie Thurston Glavin welcomed nearly 40 people to her birthday celebration Sept. 10 at the home of her son, Robert in Freeport.

Susie has lived on the Islands since she married Harley Glavin in 1924.She is originally from Sandford, Yarmouth County. The couple lived in Westport where Harley was a fisherman. He died in 1967.

In addition to Robert,the couple had two other children, Hazel and Charles. Hazel (Mrs. Arnold Titus) lives in Westport. Charles is deceased.Susie was the second person to move into the senior citizens apartment building when it opened in Freeport. She lived there for eight years before moving in with Robert and hi s wife,Leitha, several years ago.

Her talent as a quilter has gained Susie a great deal of praise from family and friends, many of whom are proud owners of a "Susie Glavin quilt." She has two on the go this fall and plans to complete them before Christmas.Susie's other favourite pastime is bingo. Leitha says Susie is at the door, ready for bingo, three nights a week. "She enjoys that very much."

Many of those dropping by the Glavin residence bring best wishes to Susie recalled the way island travel was before the road was paved. Susie recalled the way island travel was before the road was paved. Susie says she well remembers the long trip over the dirt road from Digby to Westport and the ferries used at that time.

She has happier memories of traveling by boat to Meteghan to go shopping, or to Yarmouth or Saint John when there was regular passenger service. She enjoys good health and maintains a keen interest in her grandchildren and great-grandchild, many of whom attended the birthday party.

Melbourne McDormand
Being Ninety Doesn't Slow Him Down
April 1981

A lone trick-or-treater came to the door of the Melbourne McDormand residence here last Friday evening. Mr. McDormand greeted the visitor with "What, are you out all alone? Well, I'd better go up and change my clothes and go out with you."

Though many adults enjoy seeing the costumed children at Halloween, Mr. McDormand, at age 90, seemed as delighted as the children who came to his home.

The nonagenarian was born here Dec. 8, 1890 in a house not far from his present home. He said his mother suggested he visit California during his teenage years. Later, he got a job doing private security patrol work in Pasadena, California.

"That's where I got in a scrape out there. I got married," he laughed. He met the former Callie Mae Brooks, of Oklahoma and they were married in February, 1912.The couple returned to make their home in Westport. They had two children, Edgar, of Westport and Carol, of Halifax. Mr. McDormand went fishing for a time, then became a fish buyer. Later he and his son operated a salt fish and lobster business.

The fish plant was located adjacent to the ferry wharf. Mr. McDormand said for a time he acted as agent for the steamship which used to stop here regularly. Then he decided to sell radios and later television sets and other appliances.

"Oh yes, and I was postmaster here for about 38 years," he added with a smile.He retired from active business about 15 years ago but continues to be out in the community visiting friends and relatives. He usually drives his car to the local store to do his shopping.He lives alone today in the house he helped build shortly after he was married. And the reason for his continued good health? "I've worked hard all my life,' Mr. McDormand replied.

Melbourne McDormand in 1981

Gilbert Ingersoll

Lighthouse Keeper Makes Use of Old Pump Organs
October, 1980

Gilbert Ingersoll, the keeper of Brier Island Light here, has discovered a way to give new life to retired pump organs. He dismantles them, leaving only the outside frame, then rebuilds them as china cabinets.

"The first time I made a china cabinet, I used an old ice box," he recalled. Then he tried using the pump organ for the basic frame. This was so successful, he made another. Currently he is working on one and has two more pump organs waiting to be dismantled.

"The first organ I used was in the Baptist Vestry here. I asked if they'd sell it and they said they would so I started out this way. I don't sell them, just make them for family members," he explained.

The present cabinet will have two glass doors on top, two drawers and two wooden doors on the bottom. The organ frame is usually mahogany. Mr. Ingersoll uses virola pine, a type of mahogany, to complete the cabinet. He does all the work himself in a shop near the keeper's house on the western shore of Brier Island.

"I have to be around as I'm on duty 24 hours a day now that there is only one keeper here," he said. He has been here since 1966. Before then, he was keeper of Swallowtail Light, Grand Manan for six years.

A native of Grand Manan, Mr. Ingersoll has worked as a machinist and a mechanic. He maintains a shop in the village of Westport where his services in both capacities are always in demand."I can't spend much time now in the shop," he noted. The light and fog signal are supposed to be automatic but he finds this "automatic" system does not always work.

The present red and white striped cement light was completed in October, 1944 and is 85 feet high. The original light was made of wood and lasted 130 years until it burned February 17, 1944.

Gilbert Ingersoll moved to Hartland, New Brunswick after retiring.

Gilbert Ingersoll was keeper of Brier Island Light and Alarm (Western Light) when this photo was taken. He stands with a china cabinet he made from an old pump organ.

Miss Myrna Garron
Profile of a Nova Scotian
November, 1978

In May of 1927, Capt. Charles A. Lindbergh flew non-stop from New York to Paris. In August of that same year, 16-year-old Myrna Garron walked down the dusty lane from her home here to the office of D.B. Kenney, wholesale lobster and fish dealer in Westport. Lindbergh became world famous. Myrna Garron became indispensable.

Fifty-one years at the same job, same place, same family business. Sound boring or uninteresting? "Not so," says Myrna. "It's been hectic and varied, never a dull moment, I can tell you that," she exclaimed.

Perhaps Myrna Garron made her job what it is today. A neat, well-dressed woman whose looks belie her age, Myrna has an interest in everyone and everything and a great sense of humour.   Recalling her early years with the Kenney firm, Myrna noted she started work after finishing Grade 11, "which was all they offered here at that time.

"My duties were much as they are today only there was not as much to do. The work has nearly tripled. It was a much smaller operation then," she continued.Since she hadn't studied typing or bookkeeping, Myrna taught herself these skills.

"I know I don't type exactly the way they teach you to but it works all right for me," she laughed. Auditors through the years have helped her pick up bookkeeping skills.   "For years we worked without any sort of adding machine. We did all the figuring by hand," Myrna recalled.She has more need of an electronic adding machine today because there are more figures to handle. "There were no unemployment figures to make up then, we didn't know what that was."

The payroll has increased also and this phase of her work takes the major share of her time."Now we have 30 odd boats fishing for us. When we started out we were lucky if we had half of that," Myrna noted. Boats were much smaller than those used by the fishermen here today.   "Of   course they had no radar or sounders but it seems they all used motors such as they were. They used to make a powerful noise."The fishing season ran much as it does today even though there were no government set seasons or quotas.

"But they would trawl for fish in the winter because there was none of this unemployment insurance to fall back on, they had to fish," she added.

One of the more drastic changes Myrna has noticed is in the price of lobster. When she began her career with the Kenney firm, lobsters were selling for 15 cents apiece. They weren't sold by the pound. This past winter, the going price to fishermen soared to over $3 per pound.Fish prices have also increased, though not so dramatically. Haddock today brings about 23 cents a pound to the fishermen. Fifty years ago, the price was five cents. Pollock has only gone up six cents, from four cents a pound then to 10 cents a pound today.

Living on an island used to mean traveling a great deal by boat. "When I first came to work here, they shipped by boat from here to Yarmouth or Halifax. Mr. Kenney (the late Daniel Benjamin Kenney) had his own boats but gradually we worked into trucks. Of course, Westport also had a freight and passenger service between here, Yarmouth and St. John. There were two trips a week. We'd send things that way. We thought nothing of going to St. John shopping. We all traveled more by boat than car."

The value of the dollar has especially changed since 1927. "I started working for $5 a week. No one was paid very high wages in those days but you seemed to have more than you do now," Myrna remarked.There have been many changes on the Westport waterfront. At one time there were at least five other fish dealers here. Now there is only D.B. Kenney, Ltd. The present firm is owned by the late Mr. Kenney's son and grandson.

"There were six general stores here also," Myrna noted. Now there are only two, R.E. Robicheau and the Westport Co-op. Widespread change was tragically brought to the waterfront in February, 1976. During that Ground Hog Day storm, 30 buildings were washed away. Myrna was, as usual, working in her office which extends over the water. At that time, a fish plant extended beyond the office into the harbour.

"Water started lifting the building up. Everything kept bumping into the back part of the plant as it was coming down the harbour. Before I knew it, it was pretty bad," she calmly recalled. Myrna was rescued from the office by Mrs. Danny Kenney (Theresa) who drove her truck through the rising water up to the office door. Later the fish plant was burned because it sustained major damage that day.

110

Though she can't recall ever taking a vacation of more than two weeks duration, Myrna has traveled to visit people she's met via telephone through her work. Many of these people have also come here to meet that friendly voice which has represented the D.B. Kenney firm for so long.

Hobbies? "I knit but I don't like to sew because I don't know how. I really don't seem to have time to do much else," she noted. She continues to work a five and a half day week and only during recent summers has she had any help in her office.

Myrna's many years of excellent, faithful service to the Kenney family business have not gone unnoticed. A testimonial dinner was given in her honour on July 1 by Mr. and Mrs. Danny Kenney. The guest of honour received a gold watch and a colour television set in addition to a plaque commemorating her many years of service. Many members of the Kenney family were on hand to pay tribute to their friend who has watched the family and their business grow in Westport.

Those attending the dinner included: Mr. and Mrs. Daniel B. Kenney; their son and his wife, Danny and Theresa and children, Holly and Daniel; daughter Greta Ann (Mrs. Linden Thurber) and children, Chris, Cheryl and Rodi of Bathurst, N.B.; daughter Nancy and husband (Mr. and Mrs. Roland Swift) and children, Dana, Nadene, Roland and Coralee; daughter Penny and husband (Mr. and Mrs. Roy Graham) and children, Kenney and Rosalind.Also attending were Mrs. Lorne (Greta) Swift; Mr. and Mrs. Wilfred Swift and son Ted; Mr. Alan Surette and Miss Charlotte Coche and Mr. and Mrs. Harold Robinson of Parker's Cove.

Myrna plans to continue working though she will soon be moving into a new office. Space has been reserved for her in the office in the new drying plant currently under construction near the ferry landing.Did she think she'd be at the same job for 51 years when she began her career in 1927? "No, I didn't think I'd work so long in one place but I've enjoyed every minute of it," she laughed.

Myrna retired from D.B. Kenney Fisheries in 1983. She continues to live in her own home in Westport.

Miss Myrna Garron, February, 1995 in her home, age 84.

Raymond Robicheau
Brier Island Entrepreneur
August 10,1983

"Raymond, I need a pair of boots, size 13E,"the fisherman requested."I believe I have just what you want," was the reply from the owner of Brier Island's only general store.if the customer had requested chow-chow, paint remover, pot scrubbers, panty hose, avocado pears or bicycle tires - the answer would have been the same.

Raymond Robicheau is something of a legend in this island village. If you can't find what you're looking for anywhere else, someone will inevitably ask, "Have you tried Raymond's?"

Raymond tells the story of the mechanics working on the Westport ferry. They desperately needed a vital propeller nut to get the ship back in operation. They made a trip to Yarmouth in search of the part, stopping at boat shops along the way.

No luck! They returned to Westport defeated. Word reached R.E. Robicheau."Boys, why didn't you ask me first. I have just what you're looking for!"

Raymond has been a store keeper here for 35 years. This summer, at age 60, he's taking a little time off. Two of his daughters have taken over the day-to-day operation of the store. He sat still for about an hour recently (that's his limit) to reflect upon his life.

" Not everybody is made to be a storekeeper," he began."It takes a lot of hours. You have got to stay open when the other stores are closed. Sometimes you've got to smile when you don't feel like it," he added with a grin.

He smiled when he recalled the customer who bought chocolates but asked him to mark it in her account book as bologna so her husband wouldn't know she was eating candy."You learn to know the people of the community better than the minister does," Raymond believes. "You've got to be willing to serve the people."

He began serving the people here shortly after World War II. In 1948, he bought the former A.R. Hicks store near the ferry landing because he felt there wasn't stable employment in Westport."I was born here and attended local schools until I was 13," he said.

He left for Grand Manan then and worked at the Shorecrest Lodge in North Head. His duties included escorting tourists around the island and taking the cows to the bulls. He carried suitcases and did chores. For this he received $4 a week plus Raymond went on to Saint John after two summers in Grand Manan. He worked in a hotel for $10 a week, plus board. When he was 15, he came back to Nova Scotia and worked on the night shift in Meteghan building mine sweepers.

"I left there to work on the airport at Goose Bay, Labrador for six months. I came home with $2600 in my pocket. That was good pay. We worked long hours. That was the most money I'd ever seen in my life."

He enlisted in the Army when he was 16, serving four and one half years in France, Belgium, Germany and Holland. While in Holland, he met Riekie Verburgh of Nymegen. They were married there and returned to Westport in 1946.

"In 1948, there were five other stores on the island. It was hard going for the first five or six years. Lots of time I would have to go out and do other work while my wife tended the store with the kids around her skirts," Raymond recalled.

He started right out keeping long hours. The business was open from 7:30 a.m. until 10 p.m.,weekdays and until 1 a.m. on Saturday."In those days, everybody went to the movies on Saturday night. After the movie, they'd come into the store with a big, long list. I had to fill the orders and it usually took me about two hours," he said.Three years after he opened his first store, he bought out the business across the street. "I bought the stock but not the building."

This wasn't such a good idea. Someone promptly started another store in that building so a year later, Raymond bought the stock again but this time he bought the building too! "I bought the whole works. I opened that into a pool room and canteen for the younger people. We also had a restaurant there the first year they paved the roads here, about 1955.

"I bought George Kenney's fish firm and built on to it to process salt fish which we sold to the West Indies. Two years later, I bought the E.C. Bowers fish company.

"I kept adding buildings on to what I had up here. Our present home was built to be a fish cooler. I used to drive my half-ton truck around in what is now the living room and kitchen," Raymond laughed.

One of the highlights of his fish business career was the time he had one million pounds of Newfoundland cod land in Westport between Christmas and New Year's.We didn't lose any of it. We had it all under cover by the

114

next day. I hired anyone who came along."

Raymond continued to accumulate local businesses, buying two more general stores and a dry goods store. Then the fish business began to go "down hill." "Government rules and regulations made it impossible to make a profit. Collecting unpaid bills was another problem."He consolidated his businesses into one, the E.C. Bowers Store. "By then there was just my store and the Westport Co-op," he adds.

Raymond and Riekie were really living a hectic life by this time. They had nine children, seven girls and two boys. He laughs when he recalls the night he went rushing out of the pool room and jumped into his four-door sedan. "It took me a few minutes to realize I'd leaped into the back seat!"

"The fast pace the couple kept went into even higher gear when Raymond opened two more pool rooms, one in Freeport and another in Tiverton."Pool rooms and places like that are very, very popular right in the first of it. Then later they didn't make enough money so I closed them out.."

The restaurant was eventually closed also because he couldn't find the right person to run it. When businesses slowed at his first store, Riekie took over. Raymond went pollock seining with Ray McDormand."That's what gave me the idea to go into the fish business," Raymond noted."I decided that would be a good business to get into because we couldn't sell the fish we caught."There were six fish firms in Westport at that time: E.C. Bowers, D.B. Kenney, MacLaughlin Brothers, Melbourne McDormand, Ray Rapole and Wilfred Dakin. "They couldn't begin to handle the fish that were caught," Raymond recalled.

Loses everything in storm

He was dealt a severe blow in 1976 when the Groundhog Storm washed away his store and both fish firms in about one hour. "I lost the stock, buildings, the works. I had a $212,000 loss," he states.

"I never even had 15 cents in a bank account. We were paying cash for everything. Everything we made went right back into the business.He says he soon discovered how many good friends the family had. "People were down on the beach right after the storm carrying baskets full of stuff up the beach for me. Many paid what they figured they owed me. I'd lost all the bills. One person gave me $700 and said he'd take it up in trade."

Raymond says he wondered if it would be worth the effort to open another store. "My kids said, 'Dad, you've got to start up again.' and a customer told me, 'You've got to open up, we need a second store here.'"

Two days after the storm, R.E. Robicheau was in business again selling bread and milk. Working from temporary quarters, he offered canned food without labels for $5 a box. People found many surprises when they opened what they thought was peaches and discovered peas! He moved to his present location later that year. His has been the only store here since February, 1982. He notes general stores are rapidly disappearing from Digby Neck and the Islands."If the local people don't patronize the local stores, there will be a day when there will be no stores on the Neck and Islands," he predicts.

Put it on the bill

Shopping away from home is not the only change Raymond has seen over the years. "People want things in fancy packages today. I used to put up sugar, peanuts, oatmeal in brown paper bags. Now they wouldn't buy it if you had it that way.They used to come with wheelbarrows and carts for groceries. Now they call on the phone."

People still like to say "put it on the bill." That hasn't changed but Raymond finds the credit situation is better today. "It's not as bad now as it used to be. I've always given credit. Some people are insulted if you don't. We used to carry people through the winter before there was UIC. That's what pretty near broke me. I had to sell off part of my stock to pay the bank once. The bank manager asked, "Do you think I'm Santa Claus?'"

Along with credit, people expect service. "I've had a person call down and want me to run up a box of toothpicks," he laughed.

Raymond hopes his daughters, Rikki Bolstead and Ruth Ellen Robicheau will keep the family store going. Those who know Raymond can't picture him retiring completely. He sways he will continue as agent for the Clare Mutual Fire Insurance firm, a job he's had since 1948. "It will give me something to do," he adds.He believes there's no need for all the unemployment today. The man who used to sell frost fish for 10 cents a dozen and mow lawns at 35 cents a lawn says people are too fussy about what they want to do.

":The all want to be executives. A lot of the younger people look to the government to find them a job."I still say as old as I am, I could go out and find work of some kind. I could find some way of making some money."

Meanwhile back at the store.. "Raymond, I'm trying to find a needle for my 1940 model sewing machine," a customer begins."My dear, I have just what you're looking for," Raymond replies.

Raymond Robicheau's daughter Ruth Ellen operates the general store now. Raymond continues to serve as insurance agent for Clare Mutual.

Raymond Robicheau in 1983

Ruth Ellen Robicheau, 1995. Owner of R.E.Robicheau Ltd.

Raymond with his daughter, Joyce Devries in the store, 1993.

Holland Titus
An Undertaker, a Fisherman and a Ferryman
January 4, 1984

One man worked 24 years in the undertaking business. Another man spent many years fishing. The third operated a passenger ferry between Westport and Meteghan. They meet each day to reminisce and work on crafts at the Digby New Horizon Club.

Waters Comeau, 83 was making a small wooden horse last week. He brought out brightly painted horses and wagons, horses with a hat rack and a team with a bobsled.

"I used that type of rig to haul wood when I lived in Rossway," he recalled.He said he fished out of Gulliver's Cove all his life and "that's a hard place to fish out of."

Waters moved to Digby when he retired and now lives in the Hillside Apartments with his wife, Winifred.He pays close attention to tiny details on the items he makes. He said he enjoys making his wooden crafts that are sold at the Club to help meet expenses of the organization

.Working beside Mr. Comeau is Dominic Melanson, 87, originally from Plympton, now living in Digby.Dominic said he has been in two World Wars, gone fishing, worked in lumber woods and been in the undertaking business."I've done everything but put on a Roman collar and preach," he laughed.

Dominic was making a macrame plant holder while he talked. He also makes doll cradles and wooden spoons."I was living on the top of Seawall Hill in 1922. That winter, I came up here to Digby and got a job working on the railroad shoveling snow. "The pulp boats were coming in at that time. I used to help unload the pulp boats, then we'd get a storm and I'd go back to shoveling snow."I did that all winter, the pulp was coming from Weymouth, going overseas."

He got involved in the undertaking business accidentally. "I helped the undertaker lay out my nephew. He died of spinal meningitis.Then the undertaker asked me to make some shelves for him. I did that and he kept me on all summer."He first worked for Stanley Keene who operated his funeral parlor in the building now known as the Morgue Apartments on First Avenue.

119

"That place burnt in 1927. Only the part down by the railroad tracks is the original old building.The first building there was used as a shoe factory for many years. They must have made shoes there for a long while because the boards upstairs were three-quarters wore off," he noted.

Dominic said John G. Rice was the first to use the place as a funeral home. "He was unhitching a horse from a wagon one day and the end of the shaft hit him on the funny bone. It turned into cancer and killed him." He said he enlisted in the Army when he was 18 and served four years overseas in World War I. He was wounded in 1918 by a shell which also hit two other soldiers.

He gestured toward Holland Titus working nearby. "His brother was one of the other men hit by that shell, "he said.Dominic also served four years in World WarII. He said he spent many years fishing out of a dory from Shelburne Cove on the Bay of Fundy.

Holland Titus, 86, had been steadily working on a small wooden boat while Dominic was telling about his life.He was born in Westport and lived there until he moved to Digby in 1975. He lives now in the Basin View Apartments.

Though he says he's not a skilled woodworker, he turns out fine wooden boats, oars, miniature lobster buoys and traps, birdhouses and small wheelbarrows.

Holland and his brother, Frank, operated the 50-foot passenger ferry KL, out of Westport from 1933-1945."We took over the ferry from Westport to Meteghan, calling in Freeport, operating daily except Sunday," he noted.

He said the ferry left Westport at 8 a.m., stopped in Freeport if there were passengers, arrived in Meteghan an hour later.The return trip left Meteghan at 2 p.m., arrived in Westport at three.

Holland said there were a lot of Americans using the ferry service during the summer."There was a bus service to Yarmouth. People would go to Meteghan, get the bus and go shopping in Yarmouth."He said the KL was named after the owners' wives, Kathleen and Leona. They stopped operating the ferry when it became unprofitable."People started doing their shopping in Digby," he explained.

He said he also worked for eight years as third mate on the Walter E. Foster, a Coast Guard buoy tender. "I worked with Capt. Burnett

Denton. We supplied the lighthouses. We also spent two winters breaking ice in Labrador.

"I stayed home for three years after my wife died. I was fishing then. It got to be too much for me, living alone in Westport, so I came to Digby." He said he enjoys making the tenders and traps at the New Horizon Club. "It keeps us occupied," he laughed.

Interior of the Westport United Baptist Church. The first service was held in the church December 22, 1850. When this photo was taken in 1990, a group was considering naming the church an official Heritage Property.

Warden Wilfred Swift Says It's a Challenge
February, 1980

Wilfred Swift has been a member of Digby Municipal Council for the past 15 years. He is now in his third term as Warden. Though he first refused to run for Council, Wilfred finally relented and beat his opponent. He has stayed on because he enjoys the job.

"If I didn't enjoy it, I wouldn't stay. It sure isn't the money, it's a challenge."He said when he first served on Council, he never thought he would become so involved in public affairs. Now he has a hard time keeping up with the many meetings he must attend.

In addition to serving on Council and attending the regular monthly meeting, Wilfred is also a member of the Municipal School Board. He is on the Board of Directors of Digby Hospital; the Regional Library and Tideview Terrace. He is one of the directors of the Annapolis Valley Affiliated Boards of Trade.

Wilfred attends an average of four meetings a week. A recent day showed meetings scheduled for AVABT, Board of Health and the Hospital. "I couldn't attend them all so I had to skip the Board of Health," Wilfred said.He doesn't skip many meetings, however. He notes he has never missed chairing a Council meeting. This statement probably means more to those who have traveled from Westport to Digby, especially in the winter.

Wilfred admits there have been many interesting trips over the years. "One night Parker Thurber and I made three trips up and down Digby Neck," he began.The problem was a storm had damaged buildings at the waterfront in Tiverton. There was too much debris for the ferry to get into the slip. Wilfred went back to Digby to wait a few hours until the problem was alleviated. They visited friends.

On the second trip to East Ferry, they found the ferry still not operating so they went back to Digby to wait awhile longer. After the third trip down the Neck, they learned the ferry would not be running until morning,

"Parker asked me if we had to go back to Digby. I said, 'Nothing doing.'" Wilfred recalled. He went to a friend's house and they found shelter for the night.

The front door was not locked so the two weary travelers went in with each choosing a chesterfield to lie on. After a time, the owner of the house yelled down from upstairs and asked who was there. The reply came back, "It's Wilfred Swift and Parker Thurber." The homeowner told the gentlemen to make themselves comfortable and he'd see them in the morning.

He remembers many ferry crossings when blue water came over the side. "The ferries have always been very accommodating to me," he noted. He hopes the legislation seeking free ferry service will be approved.

He has seen many changes during his years as councillor."When we first started in council, we were holding meetings twice a year, the last week in January and last week in May, Wilfred recalled.

"We did all our business during those two sessions which would last up to 12 days. We stayed up in Digby because in those days you couldn't get across the Passage at night. This would be about 1964. Then we started having quarterly meetings. Some would last two days. Now it's one a month because there is so much more business. Sometimes Council has to meet twice a month," he said.

Wilfred has also seen the Municipality grow. He cited Digby Municipal Airport as one project he has been involved with. "We have also opened two senior citizens apartments, in Bear River and Weymouth. Recreation has advanced a long way," he added. In addition to attending meetings, Wilfred said he has had to keep informed about many rules and regulations.

"I have had to learn about bylaws, you can't learn them all, you have to keep reading them, there's a lot I don't know yet," he commented.One room in his home here is set aside for his papers and formidable stacks of files are piled in this area.Wilfred built the house himself. He lives there with his wife, the former Maxine Welch. The couple have three grown children: Wilfred Lewis Roland, Charlene (Mrs. Winston McCullough) and Frederick Lawrence (Teddy).

He believes this will be his last term on Council. "My wife put her foot down and told me I had to step down after this term."He has many plans for retirement years. These include fishing with the boat he and his son, Rollie purchased last year. He might also take up a former hobby, wood carving. He and Maxine hope to attend their son's gradua-

123

tion from Confederation College in Thunder Bay this spring and journey on to North Bay. Ontario to visit his brother.Wilfred worked for 27 years as manager of the Co-op here so the family didn't have much time for traveling. He and Maxine did get to St. Pierre and Micquelon recently, a trip they describe as their "most exciting.""An old fellow told me if I ever had a chance, I should go there so I had the chance and I went," Wilfred said.

As representative of Digby County, Wilfred has met many celebrities and politicians. His years of public service have not gone unnoticed. He recently received a Queen's Medal.

Wilfred Swift died Oct. 27, 1988. His wife, Mackie died Nov. 11, 1986.

Warden Wilfred Swift, 1980

Donnie Moore got in a bit of difficulty one day. He is assisted by Ricky Buckman, at right, in freeing the Jeep. Photo by Thomas E.Norwood

Glenda Welch says Hello from her house on Second Street.Photo by Thomas E. Norwood

The view coming off the ferry in 1994.

For many years, the Cement Block was a favourite gathering spot for the younger generation. It was located at the head of the Government Wharf. Photo by Thomas E. Norwood

126

Carl Haycock Started Whale Watching in 1985 and The Island Began to Change
January, 1995

Carl Haycock first visited Brier Island in 1984. He was 25 years old. He met with Brier Island residents and told them there were many whales to be seen off the shores of the Island.

He said he was a "noted authority and photographer of humpback whales," and had been studying whales off Brier Island for two years. At this meeting, Carl showed slides of different whales he had photographed in the area and explained about identifying individual whales by markings on the underside of their tail.

He said he had identified 25 individual humpback whales off Brier Island so far that year. He noted the humpback arrives in the Gulf of Maine in April and stays usually until November when they start moving toward the Puerto Rico area.

Carl told the people in 1985 there was still a great deal of research to be done concerning whale migration. He said when he first came to Brier Island, he expected to see some right whales but was surprised to see so many humpback whales.He noted there were at that time 25 whale watching boats going out from Massachusetts ports.

He said whale watching was a big business in that area. and predicted such whale watching expeditions could also be carried out economically in this area and would benefit the local economy.

That 1985 meeting marked the start of the whale- watching era for Brier Island. Life began to change here. The change started in 1986 when Carl and Westport resident, Harold Graham started making commercial whale watching trips. The business grew slowly at first. In recent years, it brings thousands of visitors to this area each year.

This influx of people has resulted in establishment of numerous tourist-related business and an increase in business for those already serving the public. By coincidence, Carl's whale-watching idea came at at ime when the inshore groundfish fishery was rapidly declining.The result is many people who were employed in the fishery now have jobs in businesses relating to tourism. And the whale-watching business continues to grow on both islands.

I spoke with Carl Jan. 3, 1995 in his home in Irishtown. He bought the house formerly occupied by Cora Thompson. At that time, his home was also headquarters for Brier Island Whale and Seabird Cruises. He gave me copies of the sleek brochure put out by this company he formed with Harold Graham in 1986. He notes the business was formed as a partnership, then incorporated in 1988 .A larger vessel, the 44 ft. **Cetacean Venture** was purchased. Cruises had been carried out in the Graham's lobster boat, **Kenney and Girls 5.**

In 1987, Carl and Harold received Certificates of Merit at the N. S. Environmental Awards in appreciation of outstanding service in the protection of the environment.

In 1992, the company expanded again with the addition of the 52 ft. **Cetacean Quest.** Carl notes more than 10,000 passengers went whale watching with their Company in 1993 and '94.

Carl said he has kept his American citizenship but is a permanent resident in Canada. "I consider Nova Scotia my home." He said there is some resentment among Islanders about the whale watch business but added,"there hasn't been a lot of it. No one has really been rude like that. I'm friends with everyone on the island, at least I think I am. I fit in probably because I have a lot of fishing background. I understood the people.

"On a small island like this, you really have to mind your own business especially if you are from away. Also I had a business relationship with someone on the island. I don't see the Island getting out of hand because it's been a slow growth in the industry. It makes it easier for people to accept that. But our company has created seasonal employment which is good. There's room for other whale watch businesses,"he noted.

Carl said he plans to make Brier Island his permanent home. "Especially with the Brier Island Ocean Studies project. There's a tonne of stuff yet to be done. We receive a lot of credit in many journals about whales, right whales,humpbacks. I'm now working on a 10-year report on the humpback especially."

He explained BIOS was formed in 1987 to handle the research and education programs related to whale watching. BIOS is a registered Charitable society. An Adopt a Fundy Whale program provides funds for BIOS.He offers a copy of Doane Raymond's audited Financial Statement for BIOS. The report shows BIOS had revenue of $31,292 in 1994 and expenses of $40,513. However, there was a surplus of $20,931 at the beginning of the year. With the $9,221 deducted, the end of year surplus became $11,710. The Statement notes the bulk of revenue came from the Adopt a Whale program ($15,191) with the next highest generator being "Donations, memberships and sales of buttons ($10,360.)

The Statement notes "The Society is a non-profit organization dedicated to research, education and conservation of the cetaceans, seabirds and marine ecosystem of the Bay of Fundy."

Carl said the Adopt a Whale program is "pretty famous.We realized probably over $75,000 which pays BIOS operating funds,newsletters, money to purchase equipment. When BIOS started, we had nothing. Now we have two computers, two laser printers,high quality video camera, " he said. He added donations come from all over. "People love whales,they're interested in them."The latest issue of BIOS News (Autumn '94) reports 1340 adoptions since January 1992 with 249 of those being schools.

He said he doesn't mind the solitude in the winter. "There's always something to do. I'm constantly getting letters from school kids from all over North America. They want information about whales. I send fact sheets out to each of them."

One of Carl's dreams is to see an interpretive centre for whale research located on the Western Light property which the Nova Scotia government has leased to BIOS for $1 per year for the next five years. the Doane report notes use of the property is restricted to marine research and education facility with a public interpretive centre as well as housing the offices of the Society."We have the property but now we need to raise the money to build the Centre," he said.

Carl said he attends two or three conferences each year regarding whales. He gives slide shows at schools, libraries, universities and museums. In 1994, Carl and Harold received membership into the Academy of the Atlantic Canada Entrepreneurship Association and also received awards on the Impact Category for Nova Scotia. Their cruises and research have been the subject of many feature television programs on MITV,ATV, CBC as well as numerous articles in publications throughout North America.

Kenney and Girls 5 starting a whale watch trip from the ferry slip, 1988.

Carl Haycock in his home in Irishtown, January 3, 1995. Carl came to Brier Island from Maine and ,with Harold Graham, started Brier Island Whale and Seabird Cruises.

*Bill Welch aboard the **Corn Cob** at the Lower Wharf in Irishtown, 1993*

When the whale watch boat left from the ferry slip in 1988, boarding was always interesting. Passengers started boarding the cruise boats from a floating slip in Irishtown in 1989.Photo by Thomas E. Norwood

Capt. Dan Norwood shows one of the codfish caught aboard the **Timberwind No. I** *while on a deep sea fishing-whale watching cruise in the Bay of Fundy, summer, 1994. Photo by Thomas E. Norwood*

Former Plant Worker Enjoys Fishing
June, 1991

Patsy Guier, 33, has had plenty of experience working with fish. But up until last summer, the experience was confined to handling dead fish. She'd always worked in the local fish plant on Brier Island where she lives with her husband, Steven and children, Annette, 15 and Bruce, 13.

In 1990, she changed occupations and began going handlining with Steven on their 23 ft. boat, **Big Enuf**. Now she's hooked on fishing and says she thoroughly enjoys her new occupation. Patsy says she never got seasick but did get scared a few times, "when the wind breezed up." The couple fish in the Bay of Fundy off Brier Island. Steven says they usually steam one and one-half to two hours to get to the fishing grounds.

Getting up at daybreak to start the fishing day was no problem for Patsy because she's always been an early riser. She did say the blazing sun gave her quite a sunburn."At one point, I got burned so much I couldn't even grin without my face cracking." She says she never uses any kind of skin cream to protect her face.

Though they do not carry a life raft, the Guiers do have required life jackets plus an impressive array of electronics: radar, Loran C, sounder and VHF radio. Patsy says they had to get towed in several times last summer, mainly at the beginning of the season.

"It seemed like every time when we first got fishing we would break down."

Patsy says she had Steven teach her how to use the radar and operate the boat so she is capable of bringing the **Big Enuf** back to port if necessary. She adds she hopes that day doesn't arrive. "But something could happen out there that I had to bring Steven in. I am not saying I really want to do it but I know I could if I had to."

Steven says the **Big Enuf** is a good sea boat and neither he nor Patsy are afraid of fishing in the fog. "We've gone out in the fog so thick you couldn't even see the bow of the boat," he notes. Steven and Patsy are optimistic about the upcoming fishing season. "The price is up right now. I don't know what the catches are going to be like," Steven says.

133

They plan to continue fishing with their 23 ft. boat because as Steven says, "like the name, it's big enough." They say they were able to make a decent living last summer. They averaged catches of 800-1000 pounds a day, mostly cod and pollock. They use bugs and jigs. Though they sold their fish round last summer, the Guiers say they plan to salt at least part of their catch this year.

*Patsy and Stephen Guier ond their boat **Big Enuf**, 1993.*

Hauling out the **Stella Jean**, *1994. Vance Dixon, owner on the boat; Eddie Graham and Kenney Graham.*

A winter view of Westport in 1979

Water Street showing house formerly owned by Ace McDormand.

Fish plant workers at D.B. Kenney Fisheries, 1991

Is Candy the Secret?
Profile of Nellie MacDormand
August 20, 1980

You've probably read the usual reasons why a person believes he or she has outlived contemporaries. The answers run from "I've never smoked" to "I've always had a drink of rum before bedtime."

Now Nellie MacDormand has added a new reason for longevity. She'll be 90 years old on Aug. 30 and she attributes her excellent health to the fact she has always eaten candy every day of her life. She keeps boxes of candy handy for a nibble. She doesn't care if it's a hard or soft candy, just as long as it's sweet.

"I remember when I was a kid taking hard lumps of brown sugar with me to school. Then my hands would get sticky from the sugar melting," she laughed.

Though she cautions this sweet regime might not be good for everyone, it has certainly worked well for her. She has never been a patient in a hospital nor has she ever had any serious illness. She could easily pass for 60 today. She keeps busy visiting her children who are scattered from California to Ontario.

Nellie Cameron MacDormand was born here in a house about 200 yards from her present home. Her parents, Robert and Harriet Cameron had moved here from the Yarmouth area. Robert Cameron was a fisherman. Nellie was next to the youngest child in a family of five.

She remembers when she first started school. The school was the lower part of the old Westport School, now owned by a local resident. "The roads were dirt, there was no electricity, no lamps in the school. If you were bad or didn't get your lessons finished, you had to stay until 5 o'clock and it was quite dark by then in the winter," she recalled.

Nellie said students were much less wasteful in her day. "We had a small slate to write on and a little rag to wipe it clean. Once in awhile we had a bucket of water to wash off the slates. We didn't use the paper students use today. In fact, you couldn't even buy paper like that when I went to school."

There were many general stores in Westport when she was growing up. One was quite near her house and was owned by Capt. Albert Payson. "We'd holler for him to come when we wanted to buy a penny candy. When you asked for something he didn't have, he would always say, "It'll be over on the next boat,'" Nellie said.

The "next boat" referred to the steamer Westport II which regularly plied between Westport, St. John and Yarmouth. "People shopped in St. John or sent for things from there. All our food came from St. John. People didn't go to Digby very often," Nellie revealed.

She said she made her first trip to Digby when traveling to St. John to attend her daughter, Helen's graduation from nurse's training.

Nellie married Harry MacDormand in the Baptist parsonage when she was 17. They spent their entire married life in her present home. At first Harry's parents lived upstairs in the former two-family house. She had all of her nine children in this house, assisted by the doctor from Freeport.

"In those days, you didn't tell the doctor about the baby until about two weeks before you were due to deliver. We didn't have prenatal care then. We just ate what we wanted to eat and we always nursed the babies. Many times the doctor had to row over from Freeport for the birth," she added.

She said all her children were healthy and never had any serious accidents."They did have the usual childhood diseases but in those days, we thought they had to have them," Nellie remembered.

Caring for the children was mainly her responsibility because Harry was away at sea much of the time while the family was growing up. She did the washing on a washboard, had no refrigerator, used a 98 pound bag of flour each week and says today her life has been "grand."

"I've had a good life. My children have always been good to me, especially as I have gotten older," she exclaimed.

There were 38 members of her family present last week for an early birthday celebration at the Rose Bowl in Digby. Present were five of her seven children now living: Dorma Gould, Aylesford; Leland, Kentville; Muriel Derby, Chatham, Ontario; Elsie Maclachlan, Shawville, Quebec and Robert, Greenwood.

Two daughters, Helen Cunningham, St. John and Lena Burdick, Anaheim, California were unable to be present. Nellie looks forward to many more happy years. For the past six winters, she has been flying to California to live with her daughter, Lena. She says she really enjoys flying. "It's only a two-hour flight to visit my daughter, Elsie in Quebec," she noted, indicating this great-great-grandmother looks forward to every trip.

She also spends several weeks each year with her other children but returns to the family home here during the summer. She is the oldest resident of Westport.

"Oh, yes, I enjoy life. I have a grand time," Nellie smiled. She offered a visitor a candy, one from the several boxes set out on a table.

Nellie MacDormand poses on the second-storey porch of her Water Street home. She was 90 when this photo was taken.

Nellie MacDormand Marks 99th Birthday
August, 1989

Nellie MacDormand of Westport celebrated her 99th birthday in the family home last Wednesday and says she's looking forward to the big 1 00th birthday party next year.Mrs. MacDormand was born in Westport. She moved into her present home in 1907, shortly after her marriage to Harry MacDormand.

She and Harry had nine children, all of whom were born at home. Since the death of her husband in 1968, Mrs.MacDormand has spent part of each year in Westport, spending the remaining time visiting her children.

Up until last year, she regularly flew across the continent to spend several months each winter with her daughter, Lorraine in California.She is planning a trip soon to visit daughter Elsie in Shawville, Quebec."I have had a wonderful life," Mrs. MacDormand said last week.

She said she still enjoys one of the main stays of her diet- candy. Daughter Murial added her mother received five boxes of candy for her birthday!Mrs.MacDormand suggested with a smile that all the sugar has added to her longevity."That preserves you, just like a bottle of preserves," she laughed.

Murial said her mother is able to care for her personal needs though she does have trouble seeing and hearing.

Mrs. MacDormand's memory remains keen. She recalls going with her mother in the late 1800's to see Joshua Slocum
when he presented a"lantern slide" show in the old Temperance Hall in Westport. She recalled the show cost five cents.

Mrs. MacDormand can also remember when Gypsies and native people visited Westport to trade goods. She said they camped in tents in a wooded area at the top of the hill, near the Hilltop Cemetery. She said the native people had baskets to sell. The Gypsies would come with big packs on their back, full of goods to trade or sell.

Having spent so much of her life on Brier Island,Mrs. MacDormand said she can definitely see a change in the size of the island."The island has washed away a lot,I can see a big difference," she remarked.

Nellie MacDormand died Oct. 28, 1992 in Digby at age 102.

Wally Gower sitting in front of the former Westport Co-op

Wally Gower
Westport Fisherman Remembers Florida in 1914
March, 1980

When January rolls around each year, Wallace Gower recalls that first day of 1914 when he and some fellow Westporters were fishing off the coast of Florida.

`"We were out in the two dories. Earl Denton and I was in a dory. It was calm so we couldn't use the vessel. We was down from the vessel about 500 yards. I had one of them shack knives, blade over a foot long. I caught a shark. When it came up, I cut it across his gills. They got a hollering on the vessel. I couldn't figure out what they was hollering about," Wally said.

"There was a turtle that was as big as a car. They told us to get back aboard the vessel. I cut away the shark, a ten-foot hammerhead," he concluded.

Wally was born here in 1891, one of 16 children in the family. "I started going fishing when I was seven. You couldn't keep us boys out of going to Grand Manan. We had nothing to do.Then fathers in them days, they didn't even have to speak, if they pointed a finger at you, you know what they meant. That's the kind of law they had in them days."

His first fishing trip to Grand Manan was for herring. "We was over after herring to the Grand Manan ripplings. That's a place where the tide comes up amongst deep water. We were rowing our net out across the herring which were after the shrimp. A whale came up and lifted the dory right out of the water. I shoved the oar down its blowhole," Wally said with a smile.

"They won't believe that. You can't make up damn stories like that," he added.Wally continued the whale story. "Forty years later, I heard a whale with a whistle. I believe it was that same whale with the oar down its blowhole. Fishermen said they used to hear the 'Old Whistler' when he would come up with the other whales. We'd always find fish where he was."

The events of 81 years ago come clearly to Wally. He remembers he was in the dory with his brother, Fred. "I was rowing and Fred was playing the net over," he said. He believes whales have a lot of intelligence. He tells the story about other fishermen being in "what they called skiffs, something like a dory.

"Two men shot a whale. That made the whale mad. He went by 25 vessels until he found the skiff with the two men in it who'd shot him, then he ruined the skiff."The herring they caught was salted in Westport, then shipped to the West Indies. "In them days, it was all sail. They say there were 40 sailing vessels out of here and Freeport.

"They used to come here from different parts of Digby County and fish from here. They fished on the halves in them days. They'd give the vessel half and the crew kept half. Fish was all put on a fish board to divide them up."

Wally said the vessels usually arrived back in port on Saturday. "They'd salt the fish in a quinch, quinch'em on the vessel while they was out. The fish were gutted and split and put in the hold. Then they'd put'em into hogsheads and re-salt them when they got ashore.

"The fish was mostly all traded. Nobody cared much about money. Money wasn't of any value. It was all barter. That's the way it was when I was first married," Wally said.

Wally married Alma Outhouse in 1915 when he was 24. "We were together 63 years," he said. Alma died at home last year at age 82.

"I had a good wife. Always had food on the table. You know what a wife means, don't you? She cared for me and I cared for her. As far as hard times, we had to go through it. We went through the 30's. I stayed here and sold lobsters for eight cents a pound, pollock for 40 cents a hundred weight. I had no money for seven years, nothing but trading fish for other food and I had nine children but the poor devils never went hungry.

"I'd take a load of fish over to the French shore and get enough grub to last all winter, even had molasses. I took a load of fish to Weymouth one time and by God, I came back with apples, molasses, pumpkins. Once I traded a pail of cod sounds, you know what they are, don't you? I traded the pail of sounds for five barrels of Russet apples. 'There's the tree, you can go pick'em', Johnny Robicheau told me. He was the Member then for Digby County. They made the finest kind of pies," Wally continued.

When he mentioned pies, he remembered the one he'd baked yesterday. "I'll show you my apple pie," he offered and brought forth a fine looking pie.

He said his wife taught him how to make pies but "in my own head, I had an idea how to do it." He lives alone now in the big house he moved to in the 1920's. Two of his three sons are dead. A third son, Franklin, lives nearby with his family.

"My daughter, Ruby died of cancer seven months after Alma died," Wally said. "She was snuffed out. I talked to her on the phone the night before she died. What can you say to a person like that? All I could say was 'Ruby,I'm so sorry.' She was only 62 years old, a young woman just beginning to live," he said sadly.

He has seen hard times but Wally can also recall many interesting adventures. One major event in his life was the trip to Florida in 1914 when he caught the shark on New Years Day.

"George Clements always went to Florida every winter," he began. "He said he'd like to see us join him in going fishing out of Tampa. I said I'd go. Charles Pugh said he'd go but he just wanted to get clear of the cold weather. Earl Denton and James Titus rounded out the crew. Clements called us the quintet. That was in the fall of 1913, during the crisis, the beginning of the old war. However, it came the end of November. We took a ship to Boston. They hung Earl Denton up when we got there because they said he looked like some fellow who had deserted from the Army. He was there two or three hours before we got off the boat. We went on the Merchant Marriner's Line between Boston and Philadedlphia.

"We changed into another boat at Philadelphia. We had the very best of food on each boat. Fare was only $42 from Boston to Jacksonville. We stopped in Philadelphia, it was two days before the boat was ready to sail. She had 500 passengers and believe me, I enjoyed that trip. The officers on that ship couldn't do enough for you. I used to play cards with them. One game was called King Pedro. They struck on to that. They said that was some game, though I can't recall exactly how it was played.

"From Jacksonville, we took a train, the East Coast Line to Tampa. We stayed there at a hotel. Clements found a restaurant where we could eat for 10 cents. He'd save a dollar if he could. Earl Denton said we'll go up there and see what that's like. They had a five-course meal and you could eat it. What kind of meat they had, I don't know. There was flies and Negro wenches looking at you. We never went back but we did eat it. In them days, you could get a good meal for 25 cents."

Wally said soon after arriving in Tampa, they got on a good- size sailing vessel. The first trip out lasted 10 or 12 days. "We never found no fish. We made $2. Course we had our grub, we lived good aboard the vessel. "The next trip was off the Tortugas, about 100 miles from Tampa. "We found the fish there. I think it was 22,000 pounds. We made $22. that trip. Red snapper they were," Wally recalled.

He remembers an unhappy occurrence soon after returning to port from that second trip."We were fitting out for another trip and I was putting ice in the after hold. This Russian Finn had been on a drunk the night before and was thirsty. He said, "Wally, I'd give anything for a beer right now.' I gave 25 cents to a boy to get a bucket of beer, a milk bucket, you know, over two quarts. The Finn drank it all in one swoop. The beer started him to be brave again. I kept talking to him. I said, 'Look Bill, you shouldn't stand under them hatch covers there. They're loading ice.' One of them 300 pound cakes let go and smashed his right foot all to pieces. In two days, he was dead. He died of blood poisoning. I thought I might be responsible because I bought the man the beer. We left there and went to Tarpon Springs."

In Tarpon Springs, he landed a job on a yacht. "I worked for a millionaire, one of the birds who struck oil," Wally recalled.There was nothing to do whatever. In the morning, I'd get up and shine a little brass. I got $42 a month and that was big pay.

"In April, we started out in that yacht, sailed down the West Coast of Florida. The first thing we saw when we got down to Key West was a fellow who had just caught a tarpon. It weighed over 600 pounds."

His Florida adventures ended when he returned to New York on a yacht in 1914. Wally decided to head back to Westport."I'd had a letter from home. I think I had one from Alma. I had an offer to go fishing with my brother Fred. He's been dead for 15 years," Wally added.

All of the "quintet" are dead now except Wally. "Old Charlie Pugh was the lucky guy. He met up with a man and his two sons who said, 'Mr. Pugh, you're welcome to the use of my house while you're down in Florida.' Now would you believe it? He met him on the last boat we were on. We met a lot of nice people. One man had nine girls taking them to Miami. Now what was he doing with them. You can use your own judgment on that."

Wally isn't sure what has contributed the most to his longevity. "I've had some of the hardships of a fisherman, whether that could have helped, I don't know," he wondered.

"Fishermen are the hardiest crowd and most independent crowd that lives, in my opinion. I fished alone for years and every summer I'd go pollock fishing. In that kind of fishing, I had to get up at 3 a.m. I saw to it that I had my breakfast before I got out of this house. On the other hand, a fellow going on an empty stomach, what's he gonna have?

"As far as exposure, in the fishing business, I had to take it. Whether that's done me any good, I don't know. When I got caught in a gale of wind, it didn't matter who you were."

That reminded Wally of the time he was caught in "a gale of wind." It was on that famous Florida trip. "We were coming back from the second trip, a squall come up, we was obliged to go back to sea. We two-reefed the foresail, that was all she could carry. It was one of them hurricanes.

"I had to be lashed to the wheel cause the sea was coming on all over the vessel and we got in four fathoms of water. The sand was coming up with the water. The captain says, and he was a Catholic, I guess, you could see him crossing himself. He said, 'Boys, you put'er west' then he went to his bunk. It wasn't his watch. They had two-hour watches on vessels like that.

"So we had to go back to sea. It was 15 hours before you could get back to the forecastle to get a cup of tea. After awhile, Earl Denton came and took the wheel. We were in the after part of the ship. In 36 hours, we saw a change in the wind. It moderated and we got into Tampa the next night."

In addition to his hardy living, Wally believes his good wife, Alma, also contributed to his long and happy life.

"I knew Alma for many years before we decided that we were made for each other. We had a lot of arguments, everybody has to argue. We used to have a few little spats, well, I'll tell you, there were times when I did have a drink. I'd meet up with some of the boys and she'd smell it. She didn't want me to drink. No woman wants to see her husband drink. I wasn't drinking any more than I do now," Wally commented.

He limits his drinking now to a small drink of rum every morning at 10 o'clock. It is pure rum from the West Indies with enough water added to bring it down to 40 percent.

"That's one of my foolish habits. That wouldn't be a hobby, would it? That would be a habit. I don't take no more. I only take the one. I take it for my nerves, to keep me from being shaky," Wally said.

He also sips his own wine, made from either rhubarb, currants or blackberries. "All you do is put sugar in. You know what sugar does, don't you? I don't like to brag, but I believe that I have just as good a wine as they have in the government store," he added.

Wally is happy to be able to do all his own cooking and cleaning. "I am some glad to do that, my God I enjoy it," he said.

He watches the news on TV. As for the current election: "They had a boy on a man's job and he got defeated. Look it's beyond me. I'll tell you what is going to happen eventually, you and I if we live two years, probably I won't, you will have a chance of voting for Quebec or Canada. That's what it's boiling up to as near as I can follow the news. 'Cause that Rene Levesque, he's bound to have his way. Quebec has over half of the population of Canada in numbers count."

Wally goes out nearly every day. Only bitter cold or strong winds keep him indoors. He says he's not the only one who lives alone. "There's a dozen or more on this island that lives alone. I was talking to the doctor and I says, sometimes I think it's kind of dangerous for me to live alone. The doctor doesn't agree with me. He said I was doing OK by myself.

"I've been thinking it over. I saw by the paper, there's 55 people in that senior citizen's home. Now fancy me mixing up with a crowd like that. I think myself too damn independent. I'm not going to mix up with any crowd like that. If I do wind up anywhere, it will be in a hospital," he concluded.

"I've got some of the best friends here. What leave them and go into a home? I've got some brains left. The think what's against me is getting sick, but that's against you anyway."

Wally Gower died Jan. 12, 1981 at age 89, in Digby General Hospital.

George William Clements (1852-1929) on one of his Florida trips. This photo was taken at Fort Myers, Florida after Capt. Clements had completed a 1000 mile alligator hunting trip through Central Florida. Photo courtesy G.W. Clements

Is It Really Burl Ives?
Joe Hunt Talks About His
Uncanny Resemblance
August 15, 1984

Joe Hunt is a long-time summer resident of Westport. Mr. Hunt says it's fun to impersonate."Some people think I resemble Burl Ives. I disagree with them," he noted.He proceeded to recount an incident which occurred last week at the House of Wong in Digby."I live in Maryland, sometimes in Baltimore, sometimes in Bethesda," Mr. Hunt began in a distinctly Southern drawl."The first week in June, I head for Westport and I stay in my home there until September."

He said he quite often has guests from home and feels he should show them "a little of Nova Scotia, other than just Westport."

Last weekend, his friends, Dr. and Mrs. S. Titus Kimble were house guest."I decided to take them on a short trip to see some of the mainland," he continued.

After visiting the Habitation, Tidal Power project and Fort Anne, they went to the House of Wong. "The restaurant was crowded but we got service right away," Mr. Hunt said. After eating "a delicious meal," Mr. Hunt noticed a shadow on his plate.

"I looked up and there was a well-dressed gentleman just over my right shoulder with a pen and a business card in his hand."He said,'Sir, my granddaughter would be so happy if I brought her home an autograph of Burl Ives. Mr. Ives,would you just over my right shoulder with a pen and a business card in his hand."He said,'Sir, my granddaughter would be so happy if I brought her home an autograph of Burl Ives. Mr. Ives,would you please sign this card for me so I can take it to her?'"

Mr. Hunt said he looked up at the gentleman, "And thinking very fast, I said, Sure.'"He autographed the card. The man returned to his seat. "The gentleman who had been sitting at the next table, was enjoying himself very much with his beer. He had a couple."He came over and shook my hand and said, 'Mr. Ives, I love to hear you sing. give me an autograph too?'"I said, 'Why sure I will.'"And then he asked me a question.

He said, 'Are you the real Burl Ives or are you a look-a-like?'"I answered him in the sentence, 'I'm real all right.'"

Mr. Hunt said the man then pulled a crisp, new $100 bill from his pocket and put it on the table to be autographed.Mr. Hunt said he tried to convince him he shouldn't get the bill autographed because he'd lose the signature when he spent the money."He said, 'Mister Ives, I'll never spend this $100.'"

Mr. Hunt said he signed the $100 bill then noticed there were two ladies standing nearby looking at him.One said they didn't want to bother him while he was eating lunch but noted her daughter would love "so much to have an autograph of Burl Ives.""I hope you're having a good time," the lady added.

"I said, 'You don't know what a good time I am having,'" Mr. Hunt smiled.

"I signed the autograph for both of them and they sat down. I looked at my doctor friend and said I'd better get out of the restaurant before something happens," he continued.Mr. Hunt left his friends "with their sherbert and the bill.":

On the way out, he passed their waitress. "They think I'm Burl Ives and I've been writing autographs like no one's business," Mr. Hunt informed her.

"She said, 'I've been watching you.'

"When I left, she went back to our table and told my friends, 'He's been having a good time, hasn't he?'"

"He sure has. He's spelled "Burl" three different ways: Berl, Birl and Byrl and he couldn't think of another way. He should have spelled it Burl which is the way Mr. Ives spells his name," Mrs. Kimble chuckled.

Mr. Hunt said when his friends joined him in the car, "we laughed all the way home."Mr. Hunt said his wife, Elaine, will be joining him Thursday from Maryland to spend the next few weeks in Westport.

Joe Hunt, well-known Westport summer resident.
Photo taken April, 1984.

Roughnecking on Halloween,1985. Photo by Thomas E. Norwood

Troy Frost and Clifton Titus helping contain a fire on Brier Island, 1988

Some thoughtful students at the Westport School in 1979. L. to r. are Evan McDormand, Shawn McDormand and Jason Graham

Earl Lent piles salt fish on a pallet outside Dube Frost's shop. Watching is Susanna Norwood. Photo taken in 1979. Earl worked for D. B. Kenney Fisheries for more than 50 years. He died June 24, 1992.

153

On the Waterfront.....

*Jamie Swift, l. and   Clyde Stark wait to sell their fish after a trip
trawling for haddock   in the Bay of Fundy. They are shown on
Clyde's boat, the **Muriel D.** . Photo taken s ummer, 1993.*

*Melvin Titus on the **Fundy Gypsy** fishing in the Bay of Fundy, Summer, 1993.*

New Boat Saved
Jan. 21, 1981

Quick action by the Coast Guard here last week saved a new 42-ft. fiberglass boat from severe damage. The Becky and Boys owned by Howard and John Graham was moored here along with many other boats. The 65 ft. seiner Carousel was dragging her mooring during the height of the Jan. 13th storm. The Carousel was slamming into the Becky and Boys during winds that gusted to 55 knots.

A Coast Guard crew took the Grahams to their boat on the CG 102 and the Grahams were able to bring their boat into the breakwater where it was determined there was only minor damage. Visibility at the time was so poor the boats could not be seen, only heard by villagers scanning the waterfront. It was the only incident occurring during the storm.

*Howard Graham, right, owner of the **Becky and Boys**, with Floyd Graham, centre and Derek Graham. In the Bay of Fundy, June, 1993.*

Refueling at the D.B. Kenney Fisheries shed, 1978

Ebbie and Lloyd Frost chat with Bruce Dakin in this 1984   photo by Thomas E. Norwood

Fisherman Rescued From Harbour
July 1, 1987

A Westport fisherman was rescued by the Coast Guard Thursday after his predicament was noticed by a lady looking out the window of her waterfront home. A spokesman at the Westport Coast Guard station said Albert McDormand had been out working on his boat at the mooring in Westport harbour. He was attempting to get into his punt to row ashore when he got into difficulty. He was left with his feet in the punt, the lower part of his body in the water and his hands on the rail of his fishing boat.

Janet MacLauchlan was looking out the sunporch window and noticed Mr.McDormand who was yelling for help. Janet's father, Jim, called the Coast Guard on his CB radio. The Coast Guard crew went to the scene and got Mr. McDormand fully into his punt and escorted him ashore. Other than being wet, Mr. McDormand was not harmed in the incident, the spokesman said.

Tommy Albright having a snack while loading a fish truck at the D.B. Kenney plant. Photo by Thomas E. Norwood

158

The Story of the <u>Robert and Arthur</u>

The later Terrance Robicheau was a crewmember on the freight schooner **Robert and Arthur.** Terrance told   the story this way. He said the year was 1923. It was just before Christmas. He was on the **Robert and Arthur** with Capt. Fred Moore and Percy Welch. They had a load of alcohol aboard .

Terrance said Capt. Moore ran the **Robert and Arthur** ashore at Northern Point. They let the anchors go so it would not be possible to pull the vessel off the rocks. Then it was time to unload the cargo. The story is much of the cargo was taken into the nearby woods and hidden. Some people believe there are still sealed two gallon cans of Belgian alcohol deep in the woods at Northern Point.

Many containers drifted away and went up the Bay Shore. The beverage was enjoyed by Bay Shore residents for years afterward. A large quantity of the booze was taken to a coal shed in Westport village. Enterprising residents would go under the shed in a dory, drill up through the shed floor and tap into the cans. They would have wash tubs in the dory to catch the brew as it funneled downward.

This unusual shipwreck apparently brought much pleasure to many people on Brier Island , according to Terrance. Fred Moore later became keeper of the light at Northern Point.

*Eddie Graham splitting fish on the **Fundy Gypsy**, July, 1992*

159

Captain Dies, Three Saved When
Lobster Boat Hits Ledge
November, 1993

At 6:10 p.m., on the night of Nov. 30th, the 42 ft. lobster boat **Stump Jumper II** hit Dartmouth ledge at the tip of Long Island, Digby County in St. Mary's Bay. Three crew members survived. The captain and owner of the boat, Clifton Lee Prime, 62, was thrown from the vessel and died.

The crew aboard the **Stump Jumper II** had just hauled their last string of traps at about 6 p.m. and were heading home. It was a good haul for the second day of the lobster season. Aside from Clifton, in the wheelhouse that night were Leonard Howard, his son-in-law; Gregory Stark, who has been fishing with Clifton for the past 16 years and Kendall Ossinger, making his first trip of the season aboard the **Stump Jumper II**.

On most trips, Clifton would have swung his boat toward the western side of Peter's Island which divides the passage between Long and Brier Islands at St. Mary's Bay. Known locally as the little passage, it would have been the quickest route to Westport, where they would have gotten fuel at D.B. Kenney Fisheries .

But after conversations on the VHF, Clifton learned there were already several boats waiting to get fuel there, so he decided to head to Freeport instead to put his lobsters in a car. That route took him through the larger passage on the eastern side of Peter's Island and that meant going around Dartmouth Point. The **Stump Jumper II** struck the end of f the ledge on the first of the flood.

Capt.Roy Graham was a half-mile away, just off Big Cove Point, about to go through the little passage into Westport. On board his 41 ft. vessel **Kenney & Girls 5** with him were his daughter, Rosalind, 21; nephews Vance Dixon, 24 and Jamie Swift, 30.

Roy said he heard Clifton's call for help on the VHF. "He said he was on Dartmouth Ledge and asked if there were any boats around who could help him, We were there within three minutes. It all happened so fast," Roy said.

He said he was the first boat on the scene and when he arrived, the **Stump Jumper II** was listing to port, parallel with the shoreline and being violently rocked by the seas. He gave Rosalind a portable searchlight and sent her to the bow to keep a light on the disabled boat. At one point, while they were approaching the stricken vessel, Rosalind yelled to her father that she could see rocks beneath their own boat. Roy said he dared not go in any farther at that time.

Within seconds, a huge sea washed over the **Stump Jumper II** washing Gregory Stark over the side of the vessel. He had earlier grabbed a lobster buoy that helped him stay afloat while Roy took his boat around to pick him up.

"When we were trying to save Gregory,all we could see with the searchlight was his fingertips. When I put the boat in reverse, that made a little kick which brought him back up to the surface. The three of us brought him aboard," Roy continued.

By this time, Clinton Tinker and his brother, Clifford had arrived on the scene. Clinton had been waiting in Freeport for Clifton to arrive when he heard the distress call on Channel 6. Roy said both boats were standing by the stricken vessel when a huge sea lifted the entire boat clear of the water and set it down perfectly straight.

"You could see the whole length of the keel,'he said. Another sea knocked the stern of the **Stump Jumper II** down into deeper water. At that time, Clinton Tinker made a daring run toward the boat. The two remaining crew members on the stricken vessel, Kendall and Leonard,jumped for the rescue ship. Kendall landed amidships but Leonard only managed to grab the bow of the boat and was hanging on by his fingertips.

Roy said he told Vance and Jamie to throw a life ring to Leonard. At this point, Leonard was yelling that he could 't hold on much longer. Roy said he told him to drop from the boat and grab the life ring. "When he did, we pulled him aboard." Clifton could still not be seen on the **Stump Jumper II** at that time. Leonard was cold but otherwise unharmed.

Roy said his daughter Rosalind had told him several times during the frantic moments of the rescue that the person in the dark blue clothing did not seem to be moving. Roy said Clifton had been knocked down several times by the heavy seas and at one point did not seem to be able to get back up by himself. Eventually another wave would bring the awning and several crates down upon Clifton.

Leonard told Roy they were not able to cut their lifeboat free and could not reach their life jackets because the boat was rolling violently, being continually swept by heavy seas.Clifton's body was found about an hour and a half later amidst the debris of the **Stump Jumper II** by Roy's son, Kenney.

The body was recovered by Lloyd and Cecil Crocker of Freeport. A memorial fund has been set up for Capt. Prime's family. Donations may be made care of the Scotia Bank , Freeport, Nova Scotia.

Stump Jumper, *owned by the late Clifton Prime of Central Grove, Long Island. Capt. Prime died in November, 1993 when the Stump Jumper hit a ledge off Dartmouth Point.*

Ferry Petite Passage II also known as the Yellow Submarine.

*The ferry Grand Passage leaving from Freeport. Part of this ferry was incorporated into the **Petite Passage II**. Photo from a postcard.*

Lobster Season Ends
June 4, 1980

Lobster fishing season ended in District 4 last week and reports from the Federal Department of Fisheries indicate the spring fishery was not one of the best.Wellington Halliday, DFO in Digby said final reports from buyers are not in but it appears lobster catches from January to end of May were down 25-30 percent over the same period last year.

They had a good fall fishing season in this area and usually the trend is if you have a good fall, you don't have a good spring.Danny Kenney of D.B. Kenney Fisheries, Westport, said the spring season in his area has been bad. "We haven't bought half as many lobsters as we bought last year at this time," he said.

Mr.Kenney noted some of the fishermen who normally lobster in the spring gave it up early in the season to go trawling instead.Ted Sollows, statistician with DFO in Yarmouth, said the spring fishery for the area Tusket Islands to Port Maitland was about as good as last year.

"Some of the fishermen reported signs of increased catches in the last few weeks," he added.Mr. Sollows agreed with the thought that when there is good fishing in the fall,there won't be great catches in the spring. "You can't catch them twice," he said.Mr. Sollows said it seems to be true that when the fishermen are catching lobsters in the Yarmouth area, they don't catch them in the Digby area.,

"There's a northerly input, a downhill thing," he commented. There are elements of dynamics, hydrography and meteorology involved," he added.

He said the market lobster is between seven and nine years old. A fishing area usually reconstitutes itself within five months. "They'll be getting the lobsters in the last week in November, subject to poachers."

Mr. Sollows said there was a very significant drop in price of lobsters paid to the fishermen. This figure reached a high during January and February of $3.50 per pound. Closing price in this area was $2 per pound. Ex-vessel prices in Maine have been running between $2.25 and $2.50 per pound.

"Normally there is a preference for Nova Scotian lobsters. They are select and our prices are usually equal to or higher than those over there.

Fishermen are selling lobsters at the price of hamburger," he said.

Meanwhile, a check with Anthony's Pier 4 restaurant in Boston last weekend showed the price of a single lobster dinner to be either $11.95 or $14.95, depending on the size of the lobster. Dinner for two consisting of two stuffed lobsters is $16.95. In Digby, a local restaurant serves a pound and a half lobster dinner for $13. The spokesman at Anthony's said their prices went up $2 last month because the price of lobster had increased.

Ricky Graham, a familiar face on the waterfront. Ricky has done just about every type of fishing, from seining to handline to trawling. He can also fix engines and rebuild boats. This photo was taken at the boat haul-up in 1993.

Fish shop owned by Clyde and Peter Titus. Photo by Thomas E. Norwood

The fish shop owned by Glen and Bill Welch, 1994

The Ella B. in 1990, one of the Freeport hake fleet. Owned by Wayland Albright. Built in 1972 in Belleview Cove, N.S.

*Christopher Prime, seated and his brother, Randall on the **Little Spitter** in the Bay of Fundy, fall, 1993, trawling for haddock. Both boats pictured on this page were seen often in Westport harbour .*

167

*Heading home after a day of longline fishing for haddock. The **Fundy Gypsy** owned by Vance Dixon i s just ahead of the **Little Spitter** owned by Randall Prime. The southern shore of Brier Island is seen in the background.*

*The **Muriel D.** heads out into the Bay of Fundy. Peters Island light is seen as well as the Long Island shore. Standing in the stern is the boat owner, Clyde Stark. The Muriel D. was built in Overton, N.S. in 1965 and named after Muriel Derby.*

Setting traps off Brier Island left to r. Robbie Prime, back to camera; . Tracy Leeman, Dan Norwood. Photo by Thomas E. Norwood

*Loading traps on the **Miss Joy & Master Tom,** owned by Dougie Delaney. 1987 .Photo by Thomas E. Norwood*

Island Fishermen Object to Regulations
February 11, 1981

There were cries of "damned ludicrous" and "It's a dictatorship" at a meeting of the Islands Inshore Fishermen's Association here last month.the fishermen were complaining about the new personal licensing system which marks a fisherman as being either full-time, apprentice or part-time. These licenses, or registrations have been issued without any classification in the past to anyone age 16 or over who fishes commercially for at least 15 days a year.the new categorized fishing licenses also cost more money. The old permit cost $5. This year, the price is $20. A similar registration for the fisherman's boat has gone from $5 to $20.

The categorized fishing licenses are part of the recommendations prepared by Cliff Levelton on ways to improve the fishing industry in Canada. The report says defining entry to the fishery is one of the most "critical questions affecting licensing right across the Atlantic.

"The Report recommends categorized fishing licenses should be issued starting with the 1981 season though Freeport is still being considered by Canadian fishermen . The stated purposes of the categorized licenses are to provide for the identification of persons eligible for limited entry privileges and to more toward establishing professional status for fishermen.

Many Islands fishermen did not seem at all pleased with receiving a license marked "part-time." Raymond Thurber said it didn't seem right for a man who has fished 50 years and contributed a great deal to society to be issued a part-time license "just because he wants to slow down a little now."

Walt Titus said veteran fishermen should be able to "fish with dignity."I think it's a shame that the fishing industry has come to these straits."Fisheries Community Representative Arden Greenlaw said the license category can be appealed. The local appeal board is composed of five fishermen. The Islands group named Howard Graham as their representative to this Board.

One fisherman asked who decided the category for each fisherman. Mr. Greenlaw said this is the job of the local fisheries protection officer. Mr. Levelton spent two years talking to fishermen before making up his Report.

"He had a more favourable reaction to his report from fishermen all over than he did in Digby and Meteghan," Mr. Greenlaw added.Some fishermen attributed the higher price for the license to the cost of the added paperwork required as a result of the new licensing procedures.

Mr. Greenlaw provided copies of the Levelton Report to the nine directors of the Association: Walt Titus, Harold Graham and Albert Bailey from Westport; William Melanson, Lloyd Prime and Junior Munroe, Freeport and Bernard Robbins, Eric Outhouse and Robert Leeman, Tiverton.

He asked the fishermen to study the Report and make suggestions as to changes, if any. Fishermen have asked for participation in the fishery "and this is the best they could come up with. Now they are saying they don't want any part of this."

There is a second appeal board made up of five voting members; an independent chairman, a Federal representative, A provincial representative and two others, either independent or fishermen.

The Report also recommends discontinuing the current practice of issuing a license in a specified fishery to the vessel. Instead, Levelton said Licenses should be issued to the owner or lessee to use a specified registered fishing unit.He based this recommendation on the fact that the current method makes it difficult for younger men or women to raise the money necessary to become fully licensed operators.

Parker Thurber, president of the Association said another problem today is young men trying to enter the fishery cannot obtain the necessary license for a specified fishery.

"How are we going to have our young people become full-time fishermen? I'd like to see the whole thing in the wastebasket."In addition to discussing the report, the fishermen requested a letter go to the Minister of Fisheries concerning scallop permits for boats 45 ft. and under.They want to go scallop fishing in their traditional fishing area within seven miles of the Island shores.

Seiner Sinks in St.Mary's Bay
Sept. 22, 1980

Six men from this island village had a narrow escape early Tuesday (Sept. 20) morning when the 85-foot seiner Lady Sandra sank with a full load of herring in St. Mary's Bay. The wooden vessel went down about four miles off Dartmouth Point, bound for Saulnierville. She was owned by Comeau Seafoods of Saulnierville and captained by Walter Titus.

A bulkhead broke causing the herring to slide into the stern of the ship. The crew was unable to ready the seine skiff so they took to the ship's liferaft. They were picked up by Capt. Bradford Titus, son of Capt. Walter Titus, who was nearby with his ship, the Carousel.

The steel seiner, **Margaret and Elizabeth No. 1** from Grand Manan put a line on the lady Sandra but was only able to tow the ship three-quarters of a mile before it plunged to the bottom.

Members of the **Lady Sandra** crew are Everett Titus, Johnny Graham, Howard Graham, Doug Delaney and Reginald Titus. This is the first seine boat from Westport to be lost within recent memory.

*Tabatha Welch and Joanna Titus were fishing when this photo was taken by the government wharf, 1979. The vessel behind them is the **Lady Sandra**.*

Fishermen listen intently at meeting regarding the future of the fisheries. 1981

Becky and Boys *with a load of herring for lobster bait. Photo by Thomas E. Norwood*

Western Light on a foggy day showing the fog alarm building which has since been torn down. Photo taken in 1989 by Thomas E. Norwood

*The Coast Guard search and rescue boat **CG 102***
Photo By Thomas E. Norwood

*Waiting to sell their fish, part of the longline fleet. Summer, 1993. Boat's shown are the **Nicholas and Andrew** owned by Dean Albright and the **Titus Lady** owned by Peter Titus.*

*The **Mr. Jake** heads out to the fishing grounds with four tubs of haddock trawl. Working on gear is Vance Dixon, son of the boat's owner, Merrill Dixon. Summer, 1993.*

Fraggle Rock tied up beside Vance Dixon's shop

Eldridge "Squid" Garron stands on his boat, **Fraggle Rock.**

Eldridge "Squid" Garron Wonders About Future
April, 1993

Eldridge is 51 years old. He says he acquired the nickname "Squid" while fishing years ago with Stanley Moore. "We got into a whole lot of squid, 1100-1200 squid. Stanley started calling me Squid because we got so many squid that day. It would have been in my early teens, 14, 15."

Eldridge says he started fishing when he was about 16. He got out of school in 1957. In 1958, he started fishing for lobster with his brother, George. Later he fished with Franklin Gower, trawling, haddock fishing. Then he got his own boat, the **Gordon and Edna** which he bought from Raymond Robicheau. She was about 38 ft. long.Eldridge did every kind of fishing: longlining, lobster, drailing.

"I done lots of that, caught pretty much the same kind of fish as today. I used to salt fish but mostly sold them fresh. In the winter, we went haddock fishing most of the winter before Christmas until some time in January. We don't do that now because we don't seem to get the weather nowadays like you got then. The weather seems to have changed. It's blowing all the time."

Eldridge says he worked two summers, 1967-68 as a deckhand on the Marine Atlantic ferry **MV Bluenose** out of Yarmouth, traveling back and forth to Bar Harbor, Maine. "I could have gone on steady in 1968 but my father died and my mother was alone so I came home and went fishing again."

For many years, Eldridge fished the 35 ft. **Marlene Dawn,**named after his niece.The boat Eldridge has now is called **Fraggle Rock**. It was built in Shelburne by DesCamp and Jackson and finished by Joe "Bud" Lewis in Rossway, Digby Neck. She is 36 ft. long, 14-1/2 ft. wide, powered by a six cylinder Perkins engine. He's happy with his boat. "I'd better be because the Department of Fisheries won't let me get anything different."

Eldridge says he likes fishing and he's glad he started in the fishing business. "You have your good times same as anything else," he observed.

The future: "The way it's going right now, it don't look very good. I don't see too much for the future unless things are changed an awful lot. I think getting rid of the draggers or putting them on a smaller quota is one answer."Eldridge says he has no plans to retire.

Lil Brownie, owned by Arnold "Duffy" Titus of Westport. The boat is now resting in Bill Buckman's backyard.. Duffy retired and his son's got a different boat. Photo by Thomas E. Norwood

*Loading trawl from the ferry landing. Eldridge Garron, owner of the **Marlene Dawn** was waiting on his boat for Brian Baker to pass over the tubs of trawl, baited with squid. Summer, 1980*

Peter Titus was putting tags on his lobster traps piled on the Westport government wharf. Lobster season is District 34 opens Nov. 27. Last year, 7,740 tonnes of lobster were landed in District 34 with a value of about $68 million. The price paid fishermen last spring ranged from $6-$3. Fishermen fear opening price this fall may be in the $2.50-$3 range. There are 965 licensed lobster fishermen in District 34. Watching those unloading traps is Ray McDormand, r. Photo taken Nov. 1989.

Danny Gaudet working in the lobster pound, 1993.

Tanya McCullough Tells About Groundhog Storm
May, 1976

My name is Tanya McCullough and I am going to tell you about the storm that took place on Feb. 2, 1976. It was about 11:30 when my teacher let the school kids go home. I waited for my sister, Shevaun (9) and my two brothers, Darrell (7) and Jody (5). Then we walked home through the wind which was blowing very hard. Before we got home we met my Father and Mother. They were coming to pick us up in the car.

Our Father took us all for a drive. At that time the water was coming up the lane I live on. We couldn't go on the road we call the Front Road, down near the waterfront with the car because there was too much water.

So, we went home and my Father went out with the movie camera to take some pictures. At the time, the whole front road was in water and the shops started to go. The wharves ripped off from the shops and broke all to pieces. Then the shops went too. My Mother got worried because my Father had not come home for lunch and it was one o'clock. We kept watching out the window at the storm. Our front door flew off and scared us. Later Mom told us to put on some warm clothes. When we were all dressed, we went out and held on to each others' hands and practically flew down the lane and up the back road where my Grandparents live. When we go there, they were not home, so we went down to my Aunt and Uncle's house. We asked if they knew where Dad was and they said he was pumping out their basement and Danny's basement. I went in the room and looked out the window. They live on the front road. The road was stacked with wood and only a few shops were left and a store that used to be on the front road was gone.

A while later, one of my cousin's aunts came with some ice cream for us to eat. Then Nannie came in and stayed for awhile. When we were looking out the windows, we saw people coming with canned stuff from the store that had fallen into the water and were putting the stuff in their cars.

It was around four o'clock when my Mother, Father, Aunt, Uncle and my sister and cousins and I all went for a walk to have a look at the place. The road was torn up , there was wood from the shops piled up, telephone and hydro poles were down and there was water everywhere. It looked like an earthquake had struck.

During the storm, the water came up from Pond Cove on the back of the island and divided the island in two, down through the meadow. Also an old Indian dugout (canoe) was washed out from under the rocks at Pond Cove.

The new recreation and fire hall that was being built was destroyed. Also the Church steeple was blown over a little bit so that it now is crooked.

Then we all went home. The power was off so the house was cold. Mom put on the oven in the propane stove to help warm the house. Shevaun and I slept together and Darrell and Jody slept together that night with lots of quilts on us so we would be warm, but it was still cold. After a couple of days, Dad bought a generator to run the furnace and lights. We didn't have electricity for about a week.

It is near the end of May and they are still working to fix the breastwork and the roads aren't fixed yet. The fishermen are starting to build their shops again.

I have lived on this Island all my life. I am 12 years old. I never saw a storm like that. My father went lobstering with my uncle and he lost everything but his boat. In the summer, my Father went seining with Art Titus and they lost their seine on the beach but they got it back after awhile and they are having it fixed..

The Ground Hog Day storm, Feb. 2, 1976, struck Brier Island with a vengeance The above photos were taken by Raymond Robicheau and show just some of strength of the vicious storm..

Fundy Steamship Service

By Robert B. Powell. From the Chronicle-Herald,
1965

Since 1860, steamships of many types have been used to service the Fundy ports of Nova Scotia. Paddle wheels gave way to propellers and compound steam engines gave way to diesels. These steamships forged the link between the towns and villages of western N.S. and Saint John and so to the rail connection with the rest of Canada.

During the latter part of the 19th and first part of the 20th centuries, land travel was difficult and slow. It was quicker and more convenient to carry commodities by steamship on the Fundy than by horse and wagon on rough trails. This condition was conducive to trade between Fundy ports of Nova Scotia and Saint John.Businessmen and skippers in various towns and village of N.S. saw an opportunity for profit and service in steamship routes between these ports. Many local N.S. companies were incorporated to engage in this carrying trade.

The success of these companies depended principally on the management and the captains who commanded the steamers. The skippers of these small ships were well known along the waterfront of Saint John and the extent of their acquaintance with the personnel of the firms along the dockside regulated, in large measure, the amount of freight which was passed on to the steamers.

In the villages which lacked banking facilities, it was the captain of the steamer who cashed the lobster cheques. The captain who purchased the commodities, which merchants or individuals wanted from Saint John. He sold the butter and the eggs, fruit or fish for the best prices offered. He purchased large quantities of feed and flour, which he in turn sold to the merchants of the villages along the coast. He used every means at his disposal to have a full manifest every trip.

The companies, in most cases, received government subsidies; federal and provincial. Federal to encourage interprovincial trade and provincial to encourage development of local enterprise. In 1929, a group of Saint John businessmen made a study of these small steamboat companies operating on the Bay of Fundy. It was concluded that if these small companies could operate successfully with little management training, greater success could be attained under the direction of accomplished businessmen of the City.

So, in November, 1929, a meeting was called of interested persons of Saint John and the Eastern Canada Coastal Steamships Limited was incorporated. At another meeting of the company, the following minutes were written at the conclusion of the records:

"On motion, it was resolved that the president and the secretary of the company be authorized and required to sign, perform and execute all deeds, documents or things necessary or incidental to the carrying out of the purchase by the company of the following vessels: Majestic, D.J. Purdy, Premier, Hampton, Glenholm, Grand Manan, Ruby L. II, Granville III, Grace Hankinson, Bear River, Westport III, Linton, La-Tour, Tanker Rio Tambo, Tanker Rio Casma, Keith Cann, Wanda, Percy Cann, Elizabeth Cann and the Robert Cann."

Of the steamers purchased, the following were or had been Nova Scotian owned: Glenholm, Ruby L II, Granville III, Grace Hankinson, Bear River, Westport II, LaTour, Keith Cann, Percy Cann, Elizagbeth Cann and the Robert G. Cann.

The only steamers in the interprovinsial trade which are not mentioned in the list of the minutes are the CPR Empress on the Digby-Saint John route and the Valinda, which serviced Bridgetown, Tupperville, Round Hill and Clementsport. She carried freight wherever a cargo offered. In 1945, the steamer, after her 40th birthday, fell victim to fire and was declared a total loss.The Robert Cann, which ran from Yarmouth to Saint John on scheduled trips

The new proprietors of the steamers seemed doomed to financial failure from the beginning. Some of the causes were apparents while others were not as visible. The captains, who, in most cases were shareholders of the steamers they skippered, were keenly conscious of the annualdividends. They determined time of sailing, contacted prospective shippers, collected fares, added up the manifest, collected freight charges on delivery or charged to the shippers account and assumed personal risk of collection.

Administration, coming from those without sea experience, irked the skippers, who had been previously guided by their judgement and experience. Shareholders of the small companies had stepped lightly in criticism of the operation of the steamers. A skipper who thrilled from the challenge of a Fundy storm, was not prone to receive criticism graciously. His steamer was his command and he had learned to give rather than receive orders.

With the advent of centralized administration, this personal skipper control was lost. The orders were received from the office in Saint John by the captains and executed but the personal interest of assumed proprietorship was lost. This loss was not long in being reflected on the balance sheets and manifests.

The company had also inherited a number of steamers which had lived their normal span of life, some of which were over 20 and 25 years. These steamers were easily purchased and the price offered, in most cases were over actual value.When the ownership was removed to New Brunswick, the Nova Scotia government felt under no obligation to subsidize extensively a business venture of another province.

The first major setback to Eastern Canada Coastal came in February, 1930 when the Grace Hankinson, with the Ruby L II in tow, ran ashore on a ledge at the entrace to Petite Passage. Both boats were lost, taking the lives of both captains and two crewmen. A year later, the Linton foundered outside Yarmouth Harbour on the way to Saint John. All hands were lost.

The depression was making its imprint on traffic flow between the provinces and trucks were cutting into the inter-village and town transportation.

The Westport II, over 30 years of age, was caught in an ice floe in the Northumberland Strait. Her over-ripe timbers caved in and the Fundy veteran came to grief away from her home waters.

The Wanda was used for one season on St. Mary's Bay but proving unseaworthy for even this comparatively calm water, was laid up to rot away in Yarmouth Harbour. The Bear River was sold to Captain Darrell Cheney of Little River, Digby County. She carried freight wherever a cargo offered. In 1945, the steamer after her 40th birthday, fell victim to fire and was declared a total loss.

The Robert Cann, which ran from Yarmouth to Saint John on scheduled trips, foundered in a storm February 15, 1946. Twelve persons, including Captain Peters and the stewardess, Mrs. Jacquand, perished from exposure. Only one person survived, Captain Arthur Ells of Port Greville.

The Keith Cann and the Granville III, found unseaworthy, were beached at Musquash, N.B. to form a breakwater. The Glenholm was beached on the shores of the Saint John River, there to rot, away from the turbulent Fundy which she had defied for many years.

After the loss of the Robert G. Cann, the Eastern Canada Coastal Company dissolved and the holdings were taken over by the Saint John Marine Transport.

The Saint John-Yarmouth route was continued by the Saint John Marine Transport with the Mohawk II. But in the spring of 1965, this service was discontinued and so ended the small steamship traffic between these two points: a service which was in operation in 1875.

*Randall Titus, r. helps Darren Frost put lobster bait away. Fall, 1993. The two fish with Clyde Titus on the **Glass Tiger No. 1***

*The **Corn Cob**, owned by Bill and Glen Welch was built in 1977 in Port Maitland, N.S. Bill and Glen retired in 1994. The boat was sold and left Brier Island.*

*Floyd Graham, L. talks with his uncle, Philip and brother Roy on Roy's boat, **Kenney and Girls 5** at the Irishtown wharf, 1994.*

Fundy Gypsy Hits the Sea
May 19, 1989

Here is a story from the fishery that isn't discouraging. On May 2, the 34 ft. wooden fishing boat **Fundy Gypsy** was launched in Tiverton, N.S.

No big deal, you say? Well, the boat isn't huge, but it's paid for, and that's a big deal these days. And to top it off, the owner is only 20 years old, Vance Dixon of Tiverton.

Vance has been handlining with his father, Merrill, since he was 11 years old. He started fishing fulltime at 17, after graduating from high school in 1987. He is lobstering now with his father but plans to go fishing for hake in June from his own boat.

The hull of the **Fundy Gypsy** was built by Robert McPherson of Wallace. The boat arrived at the Dixon residence in September, 1987. Vance and his father completed the cabin and installed the engine and electronics.

The boat is powered by a V8 Olds engine and has Decca radar, Sitex Loran, and Robertson autopilot. She is 12 feet wide.Vance will be using his new boat for handlining and trawling in season. The vessel was christened by Vance's mother, Sheila..

Vance Dixon, l. talks with his brother, Orlie Dixon, right on Vance's **Fundy Gypsy** *while waiting to set haddock trawl in the Bay of Fundy, June, 1993. Also on the* **Fundy Gypsy** *is Bo Gillis.*

Just Enuf *owned by Dan Norwood, 1993*

190

*Charles McDormand's boat, **Brier Patch**, built 20 years ago by Kingsley Frost of Port Maitland. Charlie continues to fish every summer, usually accompanied by his wife, Alva. Photo by Thomas E. Norwood.*

Albert Moore helps out on Dumping Day, November,1993

Trevor Frost helps move a tub of lobsters over to the scale to be weighed at the D.B. Kenney Lobster Pound. December, 1994.

*Roger Thomas arriving at the lobster pound in his boat **Master Adam**.*
December, 1994.

Waiting to start: Contestants in the First Annual Slocum Tidal Race in Westport lined up to wait for the starting gun last Saturday. Evan Mc-Dormand, second in line from the bottom, won the two-mile race with a time of 15 minutes, 9 seconds. Photo by Charlotte Norwood

Winners in the Slocum Middys Race, August, 1989. There were four competitors and each received a prize. l. to r. are Tommy Delaney, fourth; Jess Tudor, third; Daniel Kenney, first and Becky Graham, second.

Nine Compete in First Annual Slocum Tidal Race
August, 1987

Evan McDormand, rowing a 13 ft. by 4 ft. fiberglass boat successfully defeated eight other rowers to win the First Annual Slocum Society Tidal Race in Westport, Saturday. Mr. McDormand completed the one-mile round trip from the Westport Government Wharf to Peter's Island in 15 minutes, nine seconds. Contestants had to stem the flood tide to Peter's Island, beach the boat, pick up a fish and return to the starting line.

Second place went to Johnny Graham, rowing a 15 ft.by 3 ft. fiberglass boat. Tony Thurber took third place in a 12 ft. by 3 ft. fiberglass boat.The Society contributed a $300 first prize while D.B. Kenney Fisheries contributed the $100 second prize and $50 third prize. An anonymous donor contributed a $20 prize to the only woman completing the race.

Other competitors were Robbie Denton in a 9 ft. by 3 ft. wooden boat; Thomas Norwood, rowing an 8 ft. by 4 ft. wooden boat; Caroline Norwood, in a 12 ft.by 4 ft. fiberglass; David Buckman, rowing a 12 ft. by 4 ft. fiberglass; Donnie Moore in an 11 ft. by 3 ft. aluminum boat and Kenney Graham, in an 8 ft. by 3 ft. aluminum boat.

This first annual race was initiated by Phil Shea who predicts there will be many more competitors next year. Mr. Shea said he got the idea about having the race when he was watching two sailboats and a sailboard in Westport Harbour last summer. he noticed the captains of these vessels were all older men while the younger generation seemed satisfied to drive across the land on ATV's or motorcycles.

Mr. Shea thought a Tidal Boat Race might interest more people, especially the younger generation, in rowing and sailing. Westport harbour was a maze of power and sail boats Saturday afternoon.He said next year, it is anticipated there will be a special race for younger rowers and possibly a category for female rowers. Boats will be given a handicap according to size, as is done in yacht races.

The Slocum Society Tidal Race was one of the many events which took place on the Islands last weekend as part of Heritage Days. Mem bers of the Race committee are John Carroll, George Clements, Al bert Graham, Daniel Kenney, Sr., Jim MacLauchlan and Mr. Shea. The

Society based in Port Townsend, Washington, is a non-profit, international association of sailing enthusiasts founded in 1955 to go support voyages in small boats.

Wilbur "Dube" Frost was watching Roy Graham's boat unloading lobsters at the D.B. Kenney lobster pound when this photo was taken in 1994. Dube has fished the waters around Brier Island for more than 60 years.

*Wayland Albright, r.owner of the **Lady Elaine I** with Eric Albright in the Bay of Fundy, trawling for haddock, June, 1993.*

*Coast Guard search and rescue boat Westport (formerly CG 102)This photo was taken in 1983 after the cutter had just brought the sinking lobster boat **TamTan** into port on the first day of lobster season. Photo by Thomas E. Norwood*

Searching for the Miss Patti
December 7, 1983

It's the first day of lobster season, November 28. The **Miss Patti**, a blue and white Cape Island boat with three men aboard is missing.An old boat, the engine might have failed. She should have returned to the Sandford wharf by 7:30 p.m. It was now 9:30 p.m.

The three-man crew of the search and rescue boat, Coast Guard 102 out of Westport have already towed two boats to safety today.
Capt. Henry Porter and crewmen Gordon Thompson and Franklin Gower had brought the sinking **TamTan** to the boatslip in Westport at about 6:30 p.m.

The men had time for a quick supper. Then the call came in to begin searching for the **Miss Patti**. They quickly got their ship underway.Henry has been captain of the CG 102 since he picked her up from the shipyard in Quebec in 1969. Gordy and Franklin are also veteran crewmembers. The three work smoothly as a team.Tonight they have little information to go on. As the CG 102 goes through the narrow passage into St. Mary's Bay, they discuss the known facts.

The 37-foot lobster boat had set out from Sandford wharf across St. Mary's Bay late that afternoon with another load of lobster traps. Relatives and friends had made repeated trips to the wharf to see if the **Miss Patti** had returned.When she was more than two hours overdue, they alerted the Coast Guard. A man spoke with Henry over the VHF emergency channel. He told what he knew about the **Miss Patti**.

"She's an old boat. I don't think they had any flares aboard. They have no radio and no radar reflector," he reported. He said the **Miss Patti** might have had engine trouble. He also described the area where he thought she might be.

Safely outside the passage, Henry put the CG 102 on automatic pilot. We sped through the dark waters south toward Trinity Ledge at about 15 knots. A north by east wind was blowing at 25 knots.

Henry kept in touch on the VHF with the man in Sandford. He also spoke on the radio to Fundy Traffic in Saint John, New Brunswick and Yarmouth Coast Guard Radio.He advised them of his position. He told the area where the CG 102 would be searching for the missing boat.Intermittently Yarmouth Coast Guard Radio broadcast an appeal to all mariners to be on the lookout for the **Miss Patti.**

The Halifax Search and Rescue Centre requested updated information each time the CG 102 changed its searching pattern.The crewmembers kept a lookout for the blue and white boat. No one knew for certain if the **Miss Patti** had any lights aboard. If the engine was not working, perhaps the battery was dead. This would mean a totally dark boat somewhere out there in the choppy seas.Henry scanned the green radar screen continually. Several times he asked Gordy to go outside to check out what might be a boat.

Tiny, white pinpoint dots would appear on the radar screen. Some would disappear into a shower of other white specks as the radar scanner made its sweep around the circle. Some stayed on the screen but they were only buoys or large balloons marking lobster traps.One time a white dot turned out to be a lobster boat still working in the Bay. The captain of this boat spoke on the VHF to Henry.

He said he'd seen a boat fitting the description of the **Miss Patti**. She'd been fishing just inside the Trinity Ledge buoy earlier that evening. He hadn't seen her for quite awhile. He was heading in now. Soon the white masthead light of this boat went by the CG 102 heading toward Meteghan. We were alone again, going south to a point nine miles beyond Trinity Ledge.The crew of the CG 102 were concentrating hard now on locating the missing boat. They peered out the spray-covered windows. Gordy went out on deck several times. "Can't see a thing," he'd report.

A voice on the VHF said he was on the Sandford wharf, with binoculars. He said he saw a red light offshore. "That's us," Henry acknowledged, flashing the boat's searchlight toward shore.After searching for nearly 45 minutes, he turned the boat around and started back up the Bay. This time he was inside the Trinity buoy. It was nearly 11 p.m. The weather forecast was for worsening conditions throughout the night, strong winds and rain due for the morning.

"I sure hope we find them soon," Gordy shouts.

Mrs. Porter, the captain's wife, speaks to him briefly on the VHF. He tells her they're still searching."You might as well go to bed," he adds.

She tells him goodnight. There is tension in the darkened cabin.

Henry enlarges the radar picture. He has noticed a tiny white dot on the screen that doesn't disappear. It seems to be stationary about six miles off Sandford.He changes course to head toward the dot. This might be it. He alerts Gordy. After awhile he says, "She should be just off our bow to port.""I can see a white stern ahead," Gordy yells.

Henry picks up the microphone and calls the man in Sandford on the VHF. "Does she have a white stern?" he asks."Yes, white stern and house, blue hull," comes the reply."We've got her!" Henry says tersely.Within minutes the powerful searchlights of the CG 102 are slicing through the darkness and the spray toward the disabled boat.Three men appear on deck, looking cold and tired. They squint into the light. The unlit boat is anchored, wallowing in the whitecapped waves.The stern of the **Miss Patti** is heaped with lobster traps. She is riding low in the water.

Quickly the CG 102 is brought alongside the **Miss Patti**. Gordy and Franklin are on deck getting the tow rope ready.Gordy ducks his head into the cabin to report to Henry with a grin that the **Miss Patti** would like a tow into Sandford. A crewman on the **Miss Patti** scrambles over the stacked traps to cut the anchor line.

Another crewman goes to the bow to fasten the towline from the CG 102. "Don't pull us too fast. You're liable to pull the bow out of the boat," he warns.

Gordy relays this message to Henry. We start slowly, towing the boat at about seven knots. Gordy stays out on deck to keep a watch on the tow. Franklin stands just inside the door.Henry advised Yarmouth Coast Guard Radio that the **Miss Patti** has been found and is under tow to Sandford. The crew reported they had nothing aboard to eat or drink. They said the engine had stopped about five hours earlier.

The **Miss Patti** refused to stay behind the CG 102 during the tow. She had a mind of her own and kept trying to go off to port. The man ashore spoke again on the VHF radio. He told Henry about the approach to the Sandford breakwater. The lights from this wharf were visible.As we approached the rocks outside the wharf, the CG 102 slowed and the **Miss Patti** was brought alongside.She was made fast to the rescue boat fore and aft and the two boats proceeded slowly up to the wharf. The tide was low. There was only a small amount of water around the end of the wharf. A man gestured from the top of the wharf, advising Henry to bring the boat around the corner of the breakwater where several others were moored just inside.

A circle of women stood huddled under the light on the wharf. A crewmember from the **Miss Patti** took the line from his boat. He stepped over the CG 102 and went quickly up the iron ladder to the top of the wharf.

People standing on the wharf went over to talk to him. It was now 12:30 a.m. Others yelled down to the two men still aboard the lobster boat. Several men thanked the crew of the CG 102. We went slowly out of the harbour and headed toward Brier Island across the Bay. Henry spoke on the VHF a final time to his friend ashore in Sandford. A voice came on the VHF asking Henry's last name. He is told it is Porter."I don't know you, Henry Porter, but I want to thank you for what you've done tonight," the voice said.The roar of the twin Detroit V8-71 diesels makes conversation impossible. Franklin goes below and returns with hot coffee. Henry sets the automatic pilot again. An hour later, the CG 102 is going through the passage at Brier Island. By 2 a.m., the crew has made her fast to the government wharf in Westport. The men had little rest. Early the next morning, they were off again to pull a Freeport boat off the rocks.

Coxswain Henry Porter at the helm of the **CG 102**

*The Westport government wharf in 1994. Boats shown include Frank Gillis' **Island Lady I** from Freeport and the **Lady Elaine I** owned by Wayland Albright. The larger boats are part of the herring fleet which frequently stops over at Westport during the day.*

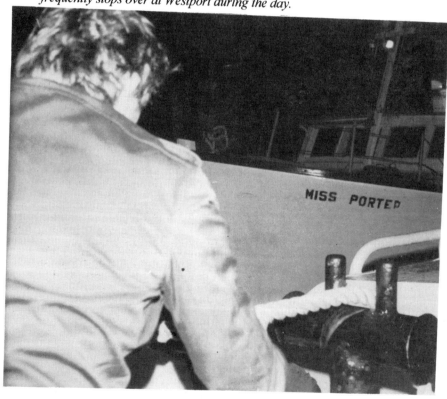

*Coast Guard crewmember Winston McCullough prepares to throw a line to the disabled **Miss Porter** on a rescue mission in St. Mary's Bay, 1983*

Marty McDormand holds a 13 pound, barnacle-encrusted lobster his father, Ray caught on a trawl off Westport several weeks ago. Marty's brother, Evan, was one of many Westport youngsters who came to look at the huge lobster. The crustacean measured two feet, six inches and was estimated to be about 30 years old. Mr.McDormand returned it to the sea. Photo taken June 25, 1980.

Profile of Ray McDormand
Another spring, another season
June, 1993

With a shy smile, 64-year-old Ray McDormand says he plans to keep fishing till he flops. I've heard of dancing till you drop, but fishing till you flop? Ray says his grandfather did just that. "He came in from fishing in his dory and he flopped."

Ray fishes out of Westport, Brier Island. He started fishing when he was 14, drailing, lobstering and trawling with his father and brother, Charley. "Drailing is out of the past today," he notes. "We towed feathered jigs behind the boat. We can't do that today, there's no fish. We haven't gone drailing around here for 10-12 years."

Ray was working on his 36-ft. fiberglass boat, **Martin and Evan II** recently. He uses the boat for lobstering, trawling and handlining. His sons, Marty and Evan, fish with their father. They started going with their father when they were three and four years old, having to stand on an oil can to steer the boat.

Ray says he's happy with the boat which was built in 1987 at the Daniels Head Boat shop, Clarks Harbour. The hull was taken to the Lewis Boat shop in Rossway where it was completed.

"I'm happy with the boat, but not with the engine, cost me pretty near the lobster season. I opened her up and she didn't slow down. The engine went to hell. We got a new one, but they didn't give it to us. Cost me $12,000."

Ray was trying to get back the GST he paid on that engine pur chase. He says it just doesn't seem right that he can't get a GST refund. He says he plans to stay in the fishery as long as there's some thing to catch, some way to make a living on the water. "I've been able to make a decent living in the past, but you can see it going down every year. I'm a jack-of-all-trades, that's if there's anything to do," he adds.

He holds three different licenses and has gone herring seining, carried herring, scallop dragging as well as lobster fishing, handlining and trawling.He never went fish dragging and thinks it would be better if there were fewer fish draggers now. He believes these draggers are one reason why there are so few fish around.

Ray has owned four other boats: the **Ray McD**; **Evelyn McD**; **Betty & Linda**; and **Martin and Evan I**. He says he doesn't see a very good future for the fishery the way it's sizing up now. Son Marty says, "unless they make some major changes in a hurry," the fishery is going to remain in a sorry state.

"There's different cycles in the fishing," says Ray. He says the only thing that saved the season around here last year was trawling for haddock, because there were very few fish for the handliners.

Ray was looking at circle hooks the day I spoke with him. He says this type of hook has come in style since he started trawling."I don't like them.They almost look like you are putting a bent hook on all the time."

One of Ray's hopes is to see a new wharf for Westport which would provide some protection and a place to tie up a boat safely.Now, nearly all the boats are kept on moorings. "It would be nice to be able to keep a boat safely at a wharf and not have to row off to a mooring in a gale of wind."

In the 50 years he's been fishing, Ray says he has enjoyed the way of life fishing offers. He has seen tremendous changes and been able to adapt to them, so far. He says he would probably retire in two years if he had enough money to do this. But he says he doesn't. That's why he plans to "fish till I flop."

*The **Martin and Evan** built in 1972 in Mavillette,N.S. The 38 ft. boat was cut up with the bow section taken to the top of Casey's Hill where it was used as a camp for several years. 1988 photo by Thomas E. Norwood*

Ray McDormand, 1993 with the Martin and Evan II

Johnnie Graham's shop and his boat, **Rebecca Louise No. 1.** *Photo taken in 1993.*

Glendon Titus
Christmas Eve on the Ferry Spray
December, 1983

Christmas Eve for Glendon Titus won't be full of visions of sugar plums. He'll have his hands full navigating the 12-car ferry Spray between Westport and Freeport. Captain Titus, ferry captain for the past nine years, goes on duty at 11 p.m., December 24. He'll be working throughout the night until 11 a.m. on Christmas Day.

"I worked last Christmas, too," he recalled. He said there is a surprising amount of traffic during holidays. "People are running back and forth between the islands visiting."

Capt. Titus will also be working on New Years Day from 11 a.m. until 11 p.m. "We work a 42 hour week, three days on, three days off," he noted. He is one of four ferry captains who live in Westport. His service on the ferry system here goes back to his teenage years.

"My father, Emerson Titus and Herman Dakin owned the ferry here. I started helping my father on the ferry when I was 15.

"I worked on the ferry until I was 18, then went on a freighter for three months, came back to Westport and started working on the **C.G. Dollard**, the old government buoy tender," he recalled.

Then it was back to the ferry for another year. In the fall of 1953, Capt. Titus joined the Canadian Army. He was in Korea in 1954, British Columbia the next year and half and sent to Egypt in the fall of 1956. Following service there with the Royal Canadian Engineers, he returned to Chilliwack, B.C. While stationed there for eight years, he met his wife, the former Lil Kroeker of Vancouver. The couple have two daughters and three grandchildren.

During his many years working on the ferry, Capt. Titus said he could only recall a few real emergency situations. "We had a bad fire once aboard the **Petite Passage II**, now the spare ferry," he said. This happened when an oil line broke, causing the engine to catch fire. "The Coast Guard was called but we had the fire out by the time they got to the ferry."

Capt. Titus said at times the routine is boring, "at times,shifts .seem to go fast. The Captain has to be in the wheelhouse nearly all the time, especially on the ebb tide." The tide around Westport drops at the rate of three feet per hour. In attentiveness could cause the ship to become grounded at the landing. Layover time in Westport between trips is about 12-15 minutes. When her husband works evenings, Lil is usually standing by the slip waiting for the 5 o'clock crossing with a hot meal for her husband.

When he isn't manning the ferry, Captain Titus takes care of about 200 chickens he has for a hobby. He says he got started raising chickens because he wanted something to do. "I was getting fat and lazy," he laughed.Capt. Titus says he never learned to swim. "The water is too cold!"

Capt.Glendon Titus on board the ferry Spray in 1983.

Island Princess Sinks
Two Rescued From Burning Boat
February 14, 1990

The 44 ft. wooden fish dragger **Island Princess** sank at about 4 a.m., Feb. 9 off Whipple Point, Brier Island after catching fire at about 9 p.m., Feb. 8 near Northern Point, Brier Island.

Cecil Crocker, owner of the **Island Princess** and Enos Comeau, both of Freeport, were bringing the boat from Tiverton to Freeport when the fire broke out in the engine room.Mr. Crocker radioed for assistance. His call for help was picked up by Westport fisherman Roy Graham who immediately alerted his son, Kenney. The two went in their lobster boat **Kenney & Girls 5** to assist the **Island Princess.**

The dragger was powerless and in total darkness in rough seas and drifting toward the rocky shore when the **Kenney & Girls 5** arrived. Prior to help arriving, Mr. Comeau had gotten in the in the liferaft but found seas too rough so returned to the dragger.

Mr. Graham managed to get the stern of his boat against the stern of the dragger so the two men could leave the burning boat. The dragger continued to burn and drifted for several more hours before sinking near Western Light. The **Kenney & Girls 5** stood by until the dragger sunk.Mr. Crocker had been talking with other fishermen on Channel 9, a VHF radio channel used by dragger fishermen.

When the fire broke out, smoke rapidly filled the wheelhouse, making it nearly impossible for Mr. Crocker to talk on the radio or change the channel. Emergency calls for assistance are usually made on Channel 16. The Coast Guard cutter **Westport** which is normally stationed in Westport, had left the night before for Mulgrave where she will be for about a month undergoing refit.

Mr. Crocker has owned the **Island Princess** for nearly 10 years. It is not known if he plans to get another dragger.Two other Westport boats, the **Becky and Boys** owned by Howard Graham and **Fraggle Rock** owned by Eldridge Garron also went to assist the **Island Princess.**

The wooden fish dragger **Island Princess** owned by Cecil Crocker. Photo taken by Thomas E. Norwood in Westport Harbour, 1988.

D.B.Kenney Fisheries plant winter, 1985 Photo by Thomas E. Norwood

Weighing lobsters at the D.B. Kenney Lobster Pound,December, 1994.
L. to r. are Susanna Norwood, Tony Titus, Roger Thomas, Judd
Howard, Arthur Titus, Dale Elliott and Trevor Frost. Mostly hidden
behind Arthur is Hartwell Sullivan.

D.B. Kenney Fisheries Expanding Once More
August 1, 1984

D.B. Kenney Fisheries Ltd. in Westport has purchased the former Point Fisheries Plant,Freeport. David Titus, general manager of Kenney Fisheries said the Freeport plant will be opening in a few weeks. It has been closed since last summer. For many years, it was operated by Connors Brothers of Blacks Harbour, New Brunswick.

Mr. Titus said there will be about 15-20 people employed initially in the Freeport Division of D.B. Kenney Fisheries. He said they will be cutting fresh filets and doing some saltfish in the Freeport plant. Mr. Titus said the Kenney plant in Westport now employs about 150 people when running at full capacity. With the additional employees working in the Freeport plant, the Kenney firm will be Digby County's major employer.

"We hope to create new employment by hiring people for our Freeport division who are not working here now," Mr. Titus stressed. He said they will be needing fish cutters and trimmers at first. "The employment figure in Freeport could grow substantially, depending upon the supply of fish available," he explained. He said there are presently seven draggers fishing exclusively for the Kenney firm."We are going to explore the possibility of bringing fish in from other suppliers." D.B. Kenney Fisheries Ltd. deals in fresh and frozen groundfish and scallops as well as saltfish and lobsters.

Daniel B. Kenney, Jr., owner of the firm, began working with his father's company in Westport in 1976. At that time, the family business was involved with saltfish and lobsters. He incorporated the present Company in 1978 and began dealing in fresh and frozen fish and scallops as well as saltfish and lobsters.

The Company has experienced continued growth during the past eight years, with many major additions to the original plant. Mr. Kenney said he got into the fresh fish business because that seemed to be the trend of the market.

"Everyone seems to want quality, fresh fish above everything else now," Mr. Kenney noted. He said his Company has always stressed quality."We stress to our dragger captains not to stay out over two days. A lot of our small draggers land fish every night. The inshore hook and line and trawl boats that land within a few hours after the fish are caught, they have the real top quality fish."

The Company sells exclusively to New England buyers. They market their product under the Brier Island and Fundy Bay brands.Mr. Kenney said one of his major buyers has visited the Westport plant many times to explain exactly what he wants in fresh fish and scallops."He has worked with us to determine how long fish will stay fresh. It is very important to know how long it takes to get the fish to the consumer and the shelf life of fresh fish," he added.

Referring to new regulations concerning dock-side grading, Mr. Kenney said that could become "a mess of worms. If we have a customer come up here and show us exactly what he wants, who else do you have to please?" he asked.. "We have come a long way with our customers. There was a lot to learn." In this part of the province, the Kenney firm buys from possibly the largest fleet of inshore fishermen."We stress looking after the inshore boats. The plant is for them. The draggers go out on the breakwater to unload," Mr. Kenney observed.

He said the Company keeps a comprehensive inventory of supplies for the fisherman, ranging from a light bulb for a running light to bilge pumps, hooks, gangions, rope, paint, boots and batteries."We are so far away from major fishing suppliers, it's important for us to have these supplies on hand for the fisherman," Mr. Kenney said.

The Company will be building a short wharf addition to the present filet plant this fall. In the future, they hope to complete a longer addition to the wharf, making a place for draggers to unload fish. The area near the plant is due to be dredged this fall.

Concerning the Freeport plant, Mr. Kenney said he didn't anticipate any problem finding additional employees. "There seems to be quite a few people unemployed." When asked the secret of keeping a small, independent fish plant prospering, he replied, "looking after it, working hard and paying attention.We don't have any trouble selling our fish. There are times when we have trouble getting enough fish, other times we don't."

D.B. Kenney Fisheries continues to operate in Westport. It is one of the very few independent fish plants left in Nova Scotia. The plant operates year-round.

Danny Kenney, owner of D.B. Kenney Fisheries, August, 1984

*Pete Titus aboard the **Just Four** in 1983. The **Just Four was** built in Cape St. Mary, N.S. in 1975. At the time this photo was taken, she was scallop fishing out of Westport. Roy Graham was captain. Pete and Jamie Swift were crew.*

An interesting front door on a house on Water Street.

One of the D.B. Kenney Fisheries trucks.
Photo by Thomas E.Norwood

An Adventure
Let's Go See the Russian Ships
August 12, 1987

Three Russian factory ships were visible from Tiverton when I crossed Petite Passage one evening last week.That was news! When I arrived home in Westport at 6:15 p.m., my husband was about to eat supper. "Let's go in the boat to see the Russian ships," I announced.His reply was, "After we eat."

By 7:10 p.m. we were underway in our 22 ft. plastic sailboat. A nice breeze from the southwest was bending the tree tops in the backyard. The breeze lasted just long enough for us to reach the narrow channel separating Brier Island from Peters Island. The tide was just starting to come in at a rate of four knots.No wind, four knot current going the other way. My husband started the outboard and we inched our way out into St.Mary's Bay. The Russian ships were not visible at first. They were 10 miles away. After about half an hour, three dots appeared.

The tide was helping us get up the Bay. The boat would surge ahead on a big sea, then the outboard would struggle to get a purchase in the water as the sea rolled under the boat. We'd sink back down in the water until the next wave lifted us high again.

After awhile, my daughter Charlotte and her friend, Marlene looked a bit bored. Charlotte had a headache. The sail flopped back and forth in the one knot wind. I suggested we should perhaps give it up and head back. "I don't know about you, but I'm going to see the Russian ships," my husband replied. We roared on at top speed - four knots.

An hour later, just as the sun was about to disappear behind Long Island, we reached the largest of the three factory ships. A blue Cape Island boat was coming from the French Shore toward the ship. This boat circled once, then let a man off at the foot of a ladder hanging over the side of the 164 m. ship.

The man climbed swiftly up the ladder and walked down the deck. The Cape Island boat came alongside us and the captain yelled, 'That's my boat." My husband said something about he must have to make big payments on it. The other people on the Cape Island boat laughed and the boat zoomed off back toward the French Shore.

We slowly circled the Russian boat. I was trying to get photos before all daylight was gone. We saw many wooden barrels piled on deck

217

Russian factory ship in St. Mary's Bay, 1987

and more in a big bin made of upended logs. There were men walking along decks on the super-structure. Many other men on the afterdecks strolled along, waving and shouting "hello" or the equivalent.

It was about 9:30 p.m. when we started back toward Westport. Actually we started toward Church Point on the other side of the Bay. The wind had come up, still a head wind, but it was at least a breeze. My husband decided to sail back but that required tacking down the Bay. The tide was against us also. It was cold, rough, spray flying occasionally rainy. On we sailed across the Bay. Brier Island seemed so far away in the growing darkness.

Finally we went on another tack that was at least taking us to the Long Island shore, somewhat below the Russian ships. After we got over that way a bit, my husband took down the sails and we began to motor toward Brier Island.By then it was total darkness with broken clouds and occasional lightning in the northwestern sky.

My husband for the first time in memory had not brought extra warm clothing. He wasn't cold but he was along way from being warm. I was dressed in the same clothes I wear in January except I didn't have any mittens. I was still cold. After an hour of pounding down the Bay, I went below to take a nap in the only sleeping bag aboard.

The floor of the miniature cabin was wet because spray had come in through the open hatch. I took off the cumbersome waterproof clothes, down-filled winter jacket, and rubber boots and folded up in the sleeping bag. The others were talking outside about lightning, rain, how rough it was, etc. Fumes from the outboard's gas tank made the cabin smell like a refinery. There is no bulkhead between the gasoline can and the cabin. With the vent open on the can, every time the boat slammed down, gas sloshed out.

Then the folding door which divides the main miniature cabin from the forward cabin came undone. It has a little rig which holds it back against the wall when not in use. It isn't exactly a Velcro strip but something like that. Every time the boat rocked or rolled, the door would crash and bang. I kept hoping one of the three people on deck would come down and push the door back. My husband did once, with a vengeance, but the door came lose again and banged some more.

I could get up and push it back but that would mean getting out of the warm sleeping bag, finding my boots, turning on the light and making my hunchbacked way into the forward cabin. Finally I couldn't stand the banging any longer so I did those things and got the darn door back. By then we were approaching Dartmouth Point and the red light on the buoy marking the approach to Brier Island.

I offered to steer. Charlotte and Marlene went down below. It was raining. I could make out dark mounds which I presumed were the rocky shores of Peters Island. My husband told me to steer for the red light at the end of the Westport breakwater. I did. He and Charlotte were standing in front keeping a lookout.

"You'd better go a little more to the left, " he advised. I moved the tiller a bit. "You'd better go a whole lot to the left," he said a little louder. So I did. At that point, he reached around to push the tiller as far over as it would go and we made a 90 degree turn away from the approaching rocks I had not seen.

The current was helping us now and we were racing back into Westport harbour. The passengers got out at the Lower Breakwater. Marlene went to her house, Charlotte and I walked home through the deserted streets. No cars on the road, nothing moving. I noticed I had put my boots on the wrong feet and that looked a little weird but I was too tired to change them. We got in the door at 11:30 p.m. My husband put the boat on the mooring and made it in by midnight. I set the clock for 5:30 a.m.and wondered whyIthink up such strange ideas. So much for my little suggestion about seeing the Russian ship.s

"But Mom, just look at it this way. We had an adventure," Charlotte observed.

*A line has been made fast to the **Doraine B.** from the **CG 102**. Also helping in the tow was the **Maranatha**, a scallop dragger owned by Capt. Edward Robinson. Photo by Thomas E. Norwood*

Dragger Grounded off Westport
July 23, 1980

The thick fog enveloping Brier Island was responsible for two accidents near here last week. A 65 ft. scallop dragger ran aground early Thursday morning. On Friday,two smaller fishing boats collided off Long Island. In a third incident, early Saturday morning a young Freeport girl was overcome by carbon monoxide while aboard a fishing boat off Gull Rock.

Capt. Henry Porter, officer in charge of the Coast Guard station here,said the Digby scallop dragger, **Doraine B.** ran aground on Big Cove Point about 2:10 a.m. while leaving the harbour here for fishing grounds in St.Mary's Bay.

He said the 17-year-old wooden vessel was loaded with 4,000 pounds of shucked and bagged scallops when she left port to complete her fishing trip. All radar equipment was working at the time but did not reveal the shoreline in close detail. She hit the rocks at ebb tide. Sea conditions were calm.

The 42 ft. Coast Guard rescue boat, CG 102 was immediately dispatched to the scene with crewmembers Franklin Gower, Gordon Thompson and Capt. Porter. initial efforts to pull the stricken ship off the rocks were unsuccessful. Capt. Porter said they were able to move the ship about 25 ft. but then the rudder apparently caught on a rock.

The crew of the dragger, including owner, Capt. Steven Robinson, Parker's Cove, had life jackets on when the CG 102 arrived but were able to step aboard the rescue boat unharmed.

Later that morning, a line similar to the fireman's "bucket brigade" was formed across the seaweed-covered rocks from the dragger to a front-end loader on the shore. The cargo of scallops was transferred to D.B. Kenney Fisheries, Westport.

About an hour before high water Thursday afternoon, the **CG 102** attempted to pull the vessel free from the rocks. Even with two 400 hp engines, the **CG 102** was not heavy enough to move the **Doraine B.** Capt. Edward Robinson, brother of Capt. Steven Robinson, joined the rescue effort with his 65 ft. dragger, **Maranatha.**

The **Maranatha**, powered by a 500 hp engine, combined with the **CG 102** to ease the **Doraine B.** off the shore.

Capt. Porter said two patches were put on the dragger while it was grounded. A pump capable of pumping 2500 gallons per hour was put aboard before the attempt was made to pull the ship free.

Mr. Thompson said some damage noted to the **Doraine B.** were the shoe torn off the keel; skeg broken;' rudder damaged; two or three holes on the bow under water; a hole on the starboard side on the waterline.

The dragger was towed to the government wharf here while a check for damage was made. When it was ascertained the vessel could withstand the trip across St.Mary's Bay to Meteghan River, the **CG 102** took her over to be repaired.Capt. Porter said there was no damage to the engine. Estimated replacement cost of the **Doraine B.** is about $500.000.

*The **Doraine B.** as she lay on the rocks on Brier Island,July 17, 1980. She grounded at 2:12 a.m. while leaving Westport harbour. She was pulled free later that dsame day and taken to Meteghan River for repairs.Photo by Thomas E.Norwood*

223

Titus Lady *going through the Passage toward St. Mary's Bay with a load of lobster traps. 1989.* ***Titus Lady*** *was built in Barrington Passage in 1987. Photo by Thomas E. Norwood*

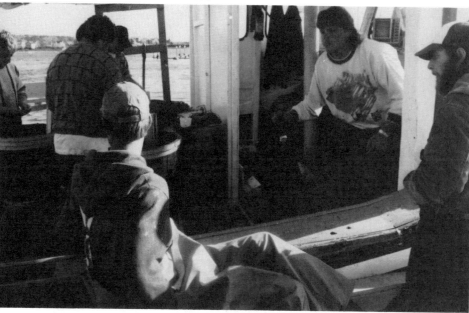

Waiting to sell out at D.B.Kenney Fisheries. Foreground are Vance Dixon, sitting, Melvin Titus,aboard the ***Fundy Gypsy.*** *On the other boat are l.to r. Christopher Prime, baiting trawl; Linden Titus,in back, and Stanley Albright. At right is the captain, Randall Prime, on board the* ***Little Spitter.*** *Summer, 1993.*

*Western Light as seen from the deck of the **Fundy Gypsy**, 1993*

*Anchored in the cove at Western Light. The **Mister Jake** from Tiverton, owned by Merrill Dixon. Trawl boats sometimes anchor in this small cove to bait up for a second set. Some older fishermen recall rowing ashore to rest in the sunshine while waiting for the tide to slack. Photo taken summer, 1993.*

*The **J.C. Karen** is framed by a fairlead on the ferry Joshua Slocum. Photo taken in 1984 when the dragger was passing through Petit Passage.*

*The **Timberwind No. 1** , owned by Vance Dixon was the first commercial fishing sailboat to fish from Westport harbour in many years when Capt. Dan Norwood started fishing with her in 1992. She was later used primarily for whale watching until she was sold in 1995.*

226

Tiverton Dragger Sinks - Three Men Rescued

Feb. 27, 1985

The J.C. Karen was a familiar   sight on the Westport waterfront for many years. She unloaded fish at D.B. Kenney Fisheries.

The 65 ft. dragger, **J.C. Karen**, owned by Small Brothers Ltd., of Tiverton, sank shortly after 8 p.m., Feb. 22 in Schooner Passage near the Tusket Islands. Those aboard, Capt. Jamie Theriault, Buzzy Hersey and Claude Westcott were rescued from their lifeboat about 45 minutes later.The dragger struck Old Man Ledge near Pease Island while returning from a fishing trip near Seal Island.

A MAYDAY was sounded by a member of the crew about 7:35 p.m. He advised Yarmouth Coast Guard Radio that the vessel was breaking up but was slowly moving across the ledge. He said he and the other two crewmembers would be taking to the liferaft when they felt they could get clear of the ledge.

The crewmember said if they had to leave in the inflatable liferaft before the dragger was clear of the ledge, there would be problems.

At 8:03 p.m., a crewmember came back into the wheelhouse one last time and told the Coast Guard, "We've got to get off now. We're abandoning ship."

That was the last word from the crew until 8:50 p.m. when the captain of the fisheries patrol vessel, **Cobequid Bay** reported "We've got the men aboard now. They are wet and happy."

Shortly after the first MAYDAY was sounded, the lighthouse keeper on Argyle Light contacted the keeper on Pease Island to see if he or any fishermen in the area could assist the stricken vessel.

Though the **J.C. Karen** was only a mile and half from Pease Island, the keeper there was unable to help because he could not launch his boat until half tide, an hour away.

A fisherman on nearby Deep Cove Island was contacted and left for the Old Man Ledge area.He arrived at the scene just after a lobster boat from Wedgeport, some 12 miles away, reported sighting a flare from the liferaft.

The captain of the **Cobequid Bay** was aboard the Wedgeport lobster boat which eventually picked up the **J.C. Karen** crewmembers.

A member of the crew said it was apparent shortly after the dragger struck the ledge that they would have to abandon ship. He said the wind was 25-30 knots from the southwest and there was "quite a swell." He noted the dragger sank about 20 minutes after they got into the liferaft.

The **J.C. Karen** was built in Meteghan River in 1977 and was formerly owned by Thurston Theriault, East Ferry.One member of the crew said the fact that the dragger was of rugged construction possibly saved their lives. He said had it been an older, weaker vessel, it would have broken up before crossing the ledge. Had this happened the liferaft would have also sunk on the ledge.

As it was, the crew jumped into the inflatable liferaft just as the dragger reached the end of the ledge, and with oars, managed to get clear of the rocks.

They drifted until they were rescued. All were wearing life jackets. One member of the crew, Buzzy Hersey said this was the fourth time he has come close to drowning while on a fishing trip.

"When you get in your first emergency situation, you learn a lot. You kind of get used to it after two or three experiences. It gives you an idea what to do," he said."I have had a little experience, even though I didn't want it," he added.

Mr. Hersey said when something like this happens, "you can't stop yourself from being scared to a certain degree. You will be scared a little bit but you have to talk to yourself and say 'we got to get out of this the best way we know how.'"

Mr. Hersey, age 34, has been fishing since he was 12 years old. He said he has fallen overboard on one occasion and been aground on vessels on three occasions. He plans to go right back to sea fishing again.

*Susanna Norwood sits on the remains of the **J.C. Karen**. This stern section washed ashore on Big Tusket Island near Wedgeport in 1984.*

Coast Guard Station Moved to Northern Point

A special meeting of the village of Westport was called Oct. 26, 1988 to discuss the proposal to move the Westport Coast Guard station from the end of the Government wharf to the lightkeeper's former residence at Northern Point. Rod Straight with Coast Guard Search and Rescue, Halifax were there, as well as Digby MLA Joe Casey, Henry Porter, Coxswain in charge of the Westport station and the Westport commissioners.

Mr. Straight said the CG 102 is here to serve an area within a 50 mile radius of Westport. Pat MacConnell, who chaired the meeting, said she and others are concerned that the boat wouldn't be able to cover a task because the crew couldn't get down the road from Northern Point. She said response time was now in seconds but would go to minutes if the base were moved.

She said she realized the crew is allowed a 30-minute time period but said going from an ideal situation to a less than ideal is something we are concerned about. "Our main concern is the road. The gravel section is extremely bad and the paved section runs through one of the most heavily populated areas of the village," she said.

Mr. Straight said the Coast Guard is replacing the eight Coast Guard buildings in Nova Scotia used by search and rescue crews. He said there is no place for a new building on the wharf. He said the Coast Guard consulted with the people in Westport regarding location of a new station. He said there are times when the wharf is pretty crowded. "We also considered the Northern Point Lightstation would be unmanned in March, 1988.

"We looked at the road. The fact normally when the lifeboat is called , the people were at their homes. Westport has the best response time in the Maritimes. We looked at where the station is located and the fact it would be good to have security about the lightstation."We have had one incident already that resulted from a flare sighting from the station. Because they were there, they were able to see what was going on," he added."Our intention will be to watch the situation pretty closely. We can bring them closer to the boat or on the boat if necessary at times," Mr. Straight said.

Henry Porter said the Westport Coast Guard has been going out to help boats for the past 19 years. "I am just stubborn enough to keep doing it. If there is a bad storm, we won't be up there. The boys will go home early but we will still be available. I am committed to going after people in that boat. Yes,we could have some problems with that road but we have alternatives. I have thought of all these things, " Henry added. He said the Westport station looks after 1,140 boats. "It is quite convenient for you to talk seconds here but for the guy off Yarmouth, it would be over two hours before we could get there. We are not always on the end of the wharf, we could be off Yarmouth."

The Coast Guard moved the Westport search and rescue headquarters to The Lightstation at Northern Point. in 1988.

The Coast Guard search and rescue base was housed in this building located at the end of the Government Wharf in Westport.

Charles McDormand was working on his boat **Brier Patch** *when this photo was taken in 1993.*

Memorable Island Meetings and Other Events...

Lightkeeper's residence at Western Light is torn down by Gilbert Ingersoll and Gordy Thompson. in 1981. Much of the material was used in other private buildings on Brier Island. Photo by Thomas E. Norwood

Unsanitary Conditions on Public Ferries

Editorial appearing in The Digby Courier, April 1 22, 1987

Last week, this newspaper carried an account of Digby MLA Merryl Lawton's Reply to the Throne Speech. In his address, Dr. Lawton praised the ferry service which operates 24 hours a day between Long and Brier Islands and Digby Neck.

We agree the ferries are reliable and the crew members courteous. But in one aspect, the ferry service provided by the Provincial government is sadly lacking.

Both ferries, the **Joshua Slocum** and the **Spray** have His and Her toilets. The toilets are flushed by a hand-operated pump. But there the "facilities" end. Neither ferry has a sink with fresh water. A health rule learned by most of us at a very early age must be ignored on these forms of public transportation.

One would think the Board of Health would have cracked down on this most unsanitary and unhealthy condition long ago. The three-man ferry crews work 12-hour shifts. This means they must eat three meals while on duty on the ferry. During their tour of duty, both the engineer and the mate must do work which in any other job would require washing their hands afterward. This includes the onerous but necessary task of cleaning both the toilets.

The mate, and on occasion, the engineer, collect ferry tickets or cash from motorists. The men are supposed to look clean and neat at all times.

This disgraceful lack of a place for both the public and the crew to wash is a black mark (no pun intended) on this otherwise fine service. We understand the crew has repeatedly asked for a small sink and fresh water supply. They received a six-inch plastic wash basin and a bar of soap for their efforts.

As more and more visitors make their way to the Islands, this lack of proper sanitary facilities becomes even more of an embarrassment. Even tiny washrooms on airplanes and buses provide a sink and fresh water for travelers.

We hope this situation will be corrected before the summer tourist season begins. Having a place to wash your hands with fresh water is a pretty basic necessity in 1987 and long overdue for these public ferries.

*The ferry **Spray** arriving in Westport, 1994.*

Government Turns Simple Task Into Costly Project
Another editorial in **The Digby Courier**-June 20, 1990

There's a problem on the two ferries which carry vehicles and passengers between Digby Neck and the Islands. It has to do with water and cleanliness. The ferries have marine toilets but no running water. Crews work 12-hour shifts on these boats with no chance to wash their hands or anything else. tourists, used to sanitary facilities everywhere else in North America, find it appalling that there is no sink nor running water in the washrooms.

This newspaper has had numerous editorials about this gross lack of sanitary facilities. Digby Municipal Council has been sending letters to the Dept. of Transportation about this matter for nearly two years.Last year, the Department spokesperson said studies were being done to determine the best way to put fresh water on the ferries. It took more than a year but "consultants" have finally come up with plans.

Unfortunately, the plans call for installation of toilets and water on the land, not on the ferries.The astronomical cost of building these facilities has prompted the Deputy Minister to ask for more plans. Now the consultants are looking into ways to get fresh water on the ferries.

On Aug.. 9, 1989, this newspaper printed a photo of the New Brunswick ferry,**John E. Rigby** which is a sister ship to the Tiverton ferry, **Joshua Slocum** At that time, we also noted this ferry has a supply of fresh water for the washrooms. The **Rigby** is 105 ft. long;, 39 ft. wide. There has been running water in the washrooms on this ferry since she was put in service in 1977. Last year, hot water was added to the facilities. The holding tank is filled once a month from a truck. The ferry has a pressure tank and pump such as is found in most rural Nova Scotia homes.

It seems too simple yet, in Nova Scotia, the government has to study the situation for over a year, hire consultants and still they can't figure out how to get a little fresh water on the ferries. This episode is typical of things done by the Government. Everything has to go through certain channels, forms have to be filled out; studies made at great cost; reports made to each level, etc. No one can just make a call to the New Brunswick Dept. of Transportation and ask them how they rigged up the tank and the pump.

Maybe by next year, after a few more reports from consultants, and great cost to the taxpayer, the Dept. will send some experts to the Islands. With any luck, within the next two years, the ferry crews and those who use the ferries will find fresh w ater in the washrooms. Then again, if the Department waits long enough, they won't need water on one of the ferries because they're supposed to have a bridge across Petite Passage by that time.

*In 1991,, both the ferry **Joshua Slocum** and the **Spray** were finally equipped with hot and cold running water at a sink and flush toilets. There is a pressure tank and a pump on each ferry.*

*Ferry **Joshua Slocum** making a crossing in heavy seas.*
Photo by Thomas E. Norwood

General Store Opens in Westport
February 15, 1989

At a time when small retailers are becoming an endangered species, a Westport couple have opened a general store. Glendon and Lil Titus are bucking the trend. Last December they opened Glen and Lil's Grocery, the first new general store to open on Brier Island in this century.

The small store on Westport's Second Street opened with little fanfare. One day there was only one store on the Island. The next day there were two."I more or less suggested we do this because on most days, there was no place for people to buy anything after 6 p.m.," Lil says.

She works as a fish trimmer at the D.B. Kenney Fish plant. She heard many of her co-workers say they'd like to be able to buy cigarettes, milk, bread and other items in the evening."We realized there was a market among those who wanted to shop evenings, fishermen especially were unable to buy things they wanted because they got in after 6 o'clock."Glendon says he thought about the store overnight, then decided it wasn't such a bad idea.

He started putting the wheels in motion the next day, calling Halifax to get a license. "When I called, they wanted a name right off. Glen and Lil's Grocery was the first thing we could come up with. It should have been something else maybe," he laughs."I mentioned it one day and came home the next and it was done," Lil recalls. They have set up their store in a former back porch of their home.

Within a very short time, their new store has grown from offering just a few convenience items to offering a full range of goods, including fresh meat, produce, subs, canned goods and a variety of ice cream treats including banana splits and ice cream sundaes.

Westport is very much home to Glendon who was born in a house just across the street and grew up on the Island. He says he knows exactly how long there has been electricity on Brier Island because he was born the year the lights came on, 1929. He left the Island to serve 12 years in the Armed Forces, then returned 24 years ago. Glendon is presently senior captain on the island ferry, Spray.

Lil is a native of Vancouver, B.C. She and Glendon and the couple's two daughters, Glenda Welch and Irma Swift take turns working in the store. Lil says they usually open for business shortly after 7 a.m. and remain open until 11 p.m. or midnight.In addition to this new business venture, Glendon recently embarked on a political career. He was elected a commissioner at Westport's Annual Meeting last week.

Wanda Graham and her daughter, Becky,shop at Glen & Lil's Store on Second Street, Westport. Serving them is Glenda Welch who took over managing the store when her parents moved from Brier Island. Photo by Thomas E. Norwood

Conservancy Vows to Work With Residents
June 14, 1989

The chairman of the Board of Trustees of Nature Conservancy of Canada assured residents of Brier Island last Saturday that the new owners of half their island want to work closely with islanders and listen to their concerns.Gordon Chaplin said the Board is very excited about the purchase of 1200 acres on Brier Island. But he added, "I don't think we pretend to have all the answers. We are going to be listening very hard to what the local people are saying.

"We are not from the government and pretend to be good guys. There's no question in my mind this will set the pace for some other things we are doing across Canada," Mr. Chaplin said.

The Trustees had been in Halifax earlier in the week to attend NCC's annual meting. Formal announcement of the acquision of the Brier Island land was made at this meeting.

Islanders asked Mr. Chaplin if the land would become a wildlife sanctuary. Gerry Glazier, executive director of the Conservancy said there is nothing formal in law about the land being a sanctuary.

"You will see very little change on the land," Mr. Glazier said. He noted however there could be a decrease in the indiscriminate use of ATV's.

"We are not here to exclude you from the land. There will be very little change," he reiterated. He said there will be signs erected designating the land as a Nature Preserve for the caring public to enjoy.

"I hope you can share in managing the land under those conditions. Legally, there will be no restrictions," he continued.

Westport Village Commissioner Penny Graham asked if the land will be fenced."We respect you people and your view points and we hope you will respect our view points," Mrs. Graham said.

"We are just a little small group of people on a very small island. I think the biggest fear is a fence. We don't want it fenced off to us," she stated.

Mr. Chaplin said it would be an impossible thing to enforce any prohibitions concerning the land and assured Mrs. Graham the NCC will not be putting up any fences."The only way this thing is going to work is with the cooperation of the people," he said.

Mrs. Graham also asked NCC to consider leasing the land to the Village of Westport should leasing ever be considered in the future. She said the Village could raise enough money to manage the land.

Mr. Glazier said an advisory board will be established comprised of a cross-section of the community.   "There is no other option but to set up the management committee," he added.

Westport teacher Jeanette Denton asked what would happen if the goals of the management committee differ from those of the NCC.

"I cannot imagine that there is going to be anything that comes down to that position but it's the landowner who has the ultimate right," Mr. Glazier said.He added Brier Island residents will be kept informed regarding any major action concerning this land.

Donnie Welch noted tax rates will go up considerably if the land is ever turned over to the Province."Do you have in your plans to turn it over to the Province?" he asked.

Mr. Glazier said initially that was the most likely ultimate objective."We have now had a chance to look at Brier Island. We think the cost of managing it ourselves would be possible. However, we have not had a recent opportunity to talk to the government about this. We have no immediate plans to make that transfer," Mr. Glazier replied.

Ms. Denton asked if the government had any "strings attached" when they gave $100,000, or nearly a third of the purchase price of the land. Mr. Glazier assured her there were no "strings attached" to the donation.

Mr. Welch asked about people cutting firewood on NCC land. Mr. Glazier said NCC wouldn't want indiscriminate cutting of firewood."We would like to be asked and grant permission," he explained.

Mr. Chaplin said NCC would be providing small maps of Brier Island which will indicate the land NCC has acquired. These will be available to the public.

A meeting of the Nature Conservancy representatives with Westport residents, July 14, 1989.

242

Liquor Store Tender Call Announced
February 4, 1981

The Nova Scotia Liquor Commission is calling tenders for a mobile liquor store to be located in Freeport. The tender call comes after an attempt by many area residents to halt the move to have a government liquor outlet on the Islands. Closing date for tenders is February 16.

Early last month, more than 200 residents of the three villages on Long and Brier Islands attended a meeting at Islands Consolidated School here to discuss the store.Digby County Municipal Councillor Parker Thurber chaired the meeting, saying he is personally against having a liquor store on the Islands.

He also said the view of the Tiverton and Freeport commissioners appeared to be any decision regarding having a store here should be influenced by the will of the majority of residents."The democratic system is going to pieces in Canada," Mr. Thurber said.

Digby Municipal Warden, Wilfred Swift, a resident of Westport, told the group he was called by the Liquor Commission and asked to meet with members in Freeport last fall."They asked me about this because I was a contact from the PC government which I am proud of," Mr. Swift stated.

He was asked his opinion about having the store in Freeport for this reason only, "not because I am Warden of the County."

He had been advised by D.W. Pulsifer, manager director of the Liquor Commission that a government store would curb bootlegging. He is personally in favour of the store because it "would make a change for the better."

The Warden said Municipal Council had received a letter from the Home and School Association and area churches stating their objection to having the liquor store here."How many letters have gone to Council about the bootleggers on each island?" he asked.

"The bootleggers are open seven days a week and selling liquor to anyone from age 14 up. I know what I am talking about, I can prove it."He said he did believe liquor is the cause of much trouble "but how much more liquor could you have than you have now?"

Tiverton head commissioner, Woodrow Outhouse said the Tiverton commissioners felt the decision about having the store here should have gone to a vote.

Henry Porter, Westport, said the first request for such a store dates back to 1970. He also noted the Liquor Commission doesn't need any vote of the Island residents in order to place a store here.Digby County voted wet in 1929.

Many attending the meeting said it was too bad to have the communities divided over the issue with neighbor against neighbor. Mr. Porter said a vote should be taken just to clear the air.

Raymond Thurber said the last report he heard plans were continuing for the store to be located behind the Riteway Store in Freeport.He wasn't very happy to learn the Commission didn't pay much attention to letters from Home and School Associations or churches.

"They said they expect to get letters against the store from those groups. They told me they had contacted the important people in the community to ask their opinion."He added the Commission said the Warden was one of the "important" people they contacted.

Islands doctor Alan Stokes said he was delighted to see such a large crowd turn out for a discussion about a liquor store. "When we had a meeting to see about having an old folks home here, ten people showed up and only one citizen attended the last annual school meeting."

Dr. Stokes said the over-the-counter sale of vanilla on the Islands is the highest in the Province. There are also brisk sales of boot polish and stove blacking."Prohibition has shown you a person seeking alcohol can always get it."

Dr. Stokes said he is in favour of having the store here because it would provide tax dollars; fulltime employment for two or three people and he would not have to drive 40 miles to get himself a bottle of beer.

Fear School Will Close
Islanders Vow To Keep Third Teacher
April 29, 1987

Nearly 100 residents of Brier Island met in the Westport Fire Hall last Thursday to protest a teacher cut made by the Digby District School Board which will leave the Westport School with only two teachers. Islanders fear this staff reduction will lower the quality of education for those students remaining in the multi-grade classrooms. They believe this move by a Board is the first step in closing the school altogether.

At issue is an island school with continuing declining enrollment and a school Board with a policy of staying with a teacher-pupil ratio of 20-1. At the Westport School this year, there are 41 students and three teachers. It cost $159,000 to operate the school lasts year and $657,000 to operate the two island schools with a total enrollment of 161 students.

Superintendent of Schools Bill Pyle compared this to another school in the District with 450 students which cost $900,000 to operate last year. Mr. Pyle said the District lost 153 students last year. "That represents over $300,000 in revenue."

When the Board moved last month to eliminate four teaching jobs in the District,the Westport School automatically became a prime candidate for one of those cuts. Islanders stressed their fear of having more students make the one-mile ferry trip across Grand Passage to attend school in Freeport on Long Island. At present, 16 students from Westport make this trip daily. An additional eight students from grades 7 and 8 make the trip at least once a week to take home economics and industrial arts at Islands Consolidated School in Freeport.

Mr. Pyle said with the teacher cut,there will be 34 students remaining in the school with two teachers instructing grades primary through six.

Concerning the issue of the ferry being overcrowded already, Mr.Pyle said there will be only six more students making the trip on a regular basis next year. School Board chairman Wilfred Swift asked if anyone believed six more students would overcrowd the ferry. Gary Frost, mate on the Westport ferry Spray quickly replied, "Yes, I do."

`It was noted the ferry has safety equipment for 76 passengers but this includes people sitting in vehicles on deck. On the days when the 25 students cross, there are no extra seats available in the cabin area. Several parents noted there are times when the spare ferry must be used. This boat has much less cabin space.

Jimmy Outhouse, a crewmember on the Spray said when the spare ferry is on. "at least half the parents allow their children to stay home rather than send them on that ferry.":Ruth Ellen Robicheau, a Westport commissioners said, "Once a cuts made,it is usually made for keeps "

"If you can do something to get the kids in the school, the teacher will come back," Mr. Swift said. He said the decision to cut the teacher was made by the majority of the School Board "and it was well discussed.."

Daniel Kenney, owner of D.B. Kenney Fisheries said he felt "this is just the start of the landslide."

Mr. Pyle said the School Board has insufficient funds to operate its education system with the staff it has now. He said the Board has to look at the Freeport School as well as Westport. He stressed the Board recognizes Westport is a unique situation. "This uniqueness is recognized every day in dollars. The School Board must take $206,000 from the students in the rest of the District to operate these two schools." He said the Westport school alone costs $72,000 a year above what the Board receives in funding from the Province for per pupil funding.

Mr. Pyle said this extra funding for the island schools "has to come from schools and students in other parts of this District." He said the two island schools have nine teachers more than the formula would allow them. "This is done with great sacrifice to other schools. " He said the School Board has no master plan to close the Westport School.

"I am not going to say that at some time in the future the Westport School will not be closed but as long as there are students to justify a teacher, there will be a school here."Mr.Pyle said the educational situation in the Westport school is not desirable, not of a standard that the School Board would recommend. He said this is not a reflection on the teachers at the school. He feels Westport students would get a better education in Freeport.

"These are known, sound educational facts. The ferry does represent an awkward and difficult situation. Our problem is we don't have enough students, " he added.He said next year there will be 16 students, grades primary through two in one room, and 18 students, grades 3-6 in the other room. He noted there are 25 potential students coming along. "If they come to school, this will tend to have five students coming in every year. This will maintain the numbers in the elementary section of the school."

Crystal McDormand asked,"Will our children be deprived by going to school in Westport?" "Educationally, yes," Mr. Pyle replied. "If I were a parent of a child in grade 6, I would think seriously about where I want that child to go to school."

When cost was again mentioned, Diane Titus, mother of two school-age children said, "Money doesn't mean a thing to me if something happens to my child on that ferry."

"I appreciate that. If a problem happens on the ferry,that is not within the power of the School Board. If there's an accident or problem on that ferry, there's no way anybody on the ferry or School Board can prevent that. That's a fact of life," Mr. Pyle stated. "The fact is,the students cross on that ferry all the time."

Board Member Nancy Villaroell said Westport is "obviously a very strong community. I would like to see if there is some way possibly we could co-operate. Working together, we might be able to come up with some solution."

One resident asked about taking a petition to the Minister of Education asking for extra funding for the Westport School. "It has been the practice that once the funding is set for the year, it isn't changed, Mr. Pyle noted. He said the Minister has not been receptive to individual pleas of this type.

"They haven't dealt with the people of Brier Island yet," Mr. Kenney noted.Walt Titus said the main problem is money and there's no concern for the children and their welfare. "This is the thing that should be looked at. Money shouldn't enter into it at all."

"What will you pay your bills with? Can you give us an alternative," Mr. Swift asked.

The following day, a petition asking the Minister for special funding for the third teacher was circulated among villagers with 190 of a possible 105 ratepayers signing the document. The petition was taken to the Minister by Digby MLA Merryl Lawton.

In January, 1988, a 44-passenger school bus began making trips to Brier Island twice a day. The bus had special safety features and each child was required to wear a life jacket while on the ferry. Later a smaller special bus was put on that run. No other vehicles are allowed on the ferry when the students cross in the bus.

By 1990, there were no grade 7 or 8 students left at the Westport School because parents chose to send their children to ICS.

Westport school "officially" became a Primary through Grade 6 school in the spring of 1994. Enrollment at the school in the spring of 1995 is 32. There are only two teachers at the school.

PROTESTING - Nearly 100 people met in the Westport Fire Hall to protest the loss of a teacher from the Westport School next fall. Many residents fear the School Board will more to close the school if teacher cuts continue. (April 1987)

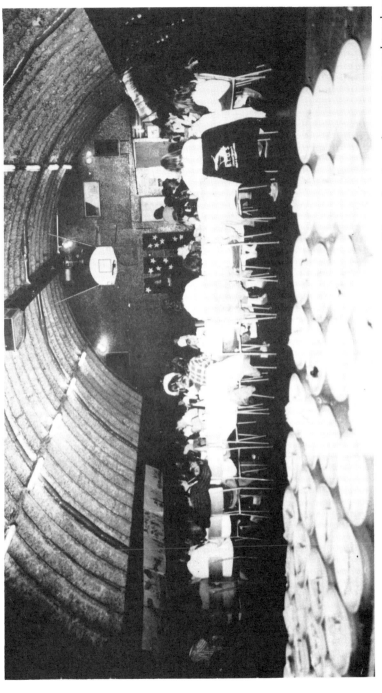

GETTING TOGETHER - Students at the Westport School prepared a Thanksgiving Dinner for themselves, parents and teachers last week. The meal was followed by entertainment by the students. The event took place in the Westport Recreation Hall. (Oct. 11, 1989) Photo by Thomas E. Norwood

*Winter scene at Irishtown wharf. When this photo was taken, boat in foreground belonged to Krista Denton.(1994) and was known locally as the **Six Pack**.*

Westport as seen from the top of the High Knoll in 1980.

Considering Link Across Petite Passage
Nov. 11, 1987

Digby MLA Merryl Lawton met with Digby Municipal Council last week at their request to discuss the idea of a causeway or bridge linking Long Island to the mainland."This idea has been around for a long time, said Dr. Lawton. "A rapid increase in tourism and fishing has lured us to the problem. It is important to get the consensus of the people living on the Island on how they feel.

"There is an attraction to living on an island that a causeway may change. It is felt a bridge would be more acceptable and desirable than a causeway," he continued. "We have to weigh the advantages of this proposal against those of the ferry service."Councillor Glen Dunn said, "We are aware of increased traffic to the Islands. We have the support of the Islands and we want to start now. Traffic signs and maneuverability should be investigated."

Councillor Ben Prince worried about people on the Islands being besieged by tourists. "We need figures on costs involved for the bridge, causeway and ferry," he noted.

Councillor Willis Marshall said a letter of support had been received from the Village of Freeport.

Dr. Lawton noted that two factors would benefit from a bridge. One would be tourism. "But we don't want a sudden influx of tourists," he said. "Brier Island is an ecologically rich area that should be preserved." Councillor Pat MacConnell commented that the ferries themselves are a tourist attraction.

Discuss Possible Link at East Ferry
Nov. 18, 1987

At a special ratepayer's meeting last Thursday, Westport residents discussed the concept of a link between East Ferry and Tiverton. Digby Municipal Councillor Patricia MacConnell said Digby MLA Merryl Lawton wanted to know the feelings of the Islanders about a bridge or causeway between Long Island and the mainland.

Several ratepayers said a bridge or causeway would be more economical than operating the present ferry service. Mrs. MacConnell said it is estimated the ferry now making this run will have to be replaced within five years. She said two factors in favour of a link are

251

Islanders would be able to have increased police protection and older residents would have easier access to Digby Hospital. Those speaking against the issue said they believed the link would cost jobs and they felt easier access to the Islands might destroy the island way of life.

Danny Kenney, owner of three major fish plants on the Islands says the debate is similar to one held many years ago. "When they had the horse and buggy, they didn't want the motor vehicle to come along and that's roughly how I feel.

"If the traffic increases next summer, I don't know where it's going to fit. It's definitely a problem for everyone," Mr. Kenney says. The Kenney firm operates a fleet of five tractor-trailer units, plus numerous smaller trucks. "If you have to make a ferry schedule, it was tough enough this summer for us. We had some very close shaves with our trucks just barely making the ferry in Yarmouth."

Mr. Kenney says being held up on ferry overloads in Tiverton could mean a 24-hour delay getting fresh seafood to the Boston market, a very expensive delay.

Westport resident Carl Haycock, an owner of the whale watching business on Brier Island, suggested a group of three go door-to-door in Westport asking residents their views on the matter. Ruth Ellen Robicheau , Glenda Welch and Irma Swift volunteered to do this task.

Roxanne Prime and Robbie Denton were just leaving the Westport Fire Hall when this photo was taken in 1993 by Thomas E. Norwood.

Bridge to Island Promised in '77

December 2, 1987

"I wish to advise that I will now be bringing the matter of the ferries across Petite Passage and Grand Passage up in the Legislature. There's no doubt in my mind that the Department of Highways has wasted a great deal of money on this service.

"I wish to advise you that the Conservative Party both on the Federal and Provincial levels recognize this problem and you may recall that Louis Comeau (when he was the Federal MP advocated a bridge and approaches from the mainland to Long Island.

"I agree with that proposition and would do everything in my power to ensure that construction of such a bridge with Federal and Provincial funds. The service to Brier Island from Long Island must be carried on with a modern 24 hour ferry. "I can assure you that this is our goal when we form the government of this Province."

This letter was written April, 1977 and signed by the Leader of the Opposition, John M. Buchanan, Q.C.

Digby Municipal Councillors had a chance to read a copy of this letter last week as well as another from the Leader of the Opposition written in November, 1976.

In the 1976 letter,Mr.Buchanan said he had received numerous complaints about the ferry service in the Digby Neck area.

"The vessel between Tiverton and East Ferry breaks down very often and on a f ew occasions has broken down in mid-stream.

This,of course, as you are aware, could be very dangerous and end up with tragic results in view of the strong tides and currents in that area."

In the year 1976, it is ridiculous that this area is not serviced by a bridge. The Government of Nova Scotia seems to be able to find money for many projects which are not beneficial, but when it comes to something as vitally important as a transportation link between the Digby Neck Islands, money just is not available.

"It seems to me every effort should have been made and should now be made to build a bridge between East Ferry and Tiverton. The present service is inadequate and not much better than that provided 30 years ago."

The letters were given to Council by Freeport resident Herbert Thurber. Mr. Thurber said he never received a reply to any of his letter about the bridge after Mr. Buchanan became Premier.

"I suppose the excuse would be that he didn't get them, although there was no problem about it when he was in the Opposition," Mr. Thurber noted.

Councillor Patricia MacConnell said a CBC-TV news broadcast about Westport resident discussing the bridge was mixed up. She said when CBC showed people voting, they were actually voting on a motion to send someone to New Zealand rather than on the issue of a bridge across Petite Passage.

Mrs. MacConnell said only about 30 people attended the Westport meeting called specifically to discuss the bridge issue. She said a majority of those present were against a bridge across Petite. She said a door-to-door survey is being done in Westport to see how other residents feel about the matter.

"If the people on Long Island really want it, there isn't any way we are going to stand up and fight it," Mrs. MacConnell observed.

Municipal Clerk Bill McMillan read a letter from the Tiverton Village Commission giving their full support to the idea of a bridge across Petite.

Councillor Parker Thurber said he believed the people in Westport will be in favour of a bridge. Council has already received a letter from the Freeport Village Commission giving their support to the bridge proposal.

In March, 1995, there is still no fixed link to the mainland. A new 18-car ferry is expected to be in service on the East Ferry-Tiverton run by June,1995. A new ferry wharf was built in Westport in 1994. The ferry Joshua Slocum will be moved to Westport when the new ferry is put in service. The Westport ferry Spray will serve as a spare ferry for the Islands.

Sunday School classes are being held in the historic Baptist Church in Westport while renovations are made to the Vestry under a $29,719 Canada Works Grant. Shown with their teacher, Shirley Roy, are l. to r. Nichole Titus, Michelle Pugh, Nicky Adams and Jason Graham. (Jan. 23, 1980)

Drier Island?
Westport Votes 'Dry'

On March 13, 1990, a vote was taken in Westport regarding the sale of liquor on the island. The vote was 97-89 against. The ballots read: Are you in favour of the sale of liquor for consumption on the premises licensed by the Liquor License Board?

The call for a plebiscite was made by Thomas Norwood who was considering opening an English-style pub in Westport. The 23-year-old resident hoped a pub would provide jobs and give residents and tourists a nice place to visit. A petition in favor was circulated before the vote. Mr. Norwood said later he believed the island would have gone wet but some residents were away on vacation and did not vote.

In a letter to the editor of the Digby Courier March 7, 1990, Rev. John Carroll, with the Westport United Baptist Church, urged residents to vote against the granting of liquor licenses. He indicated he worries about the ill effects of alcohol.

Mr. Norwood says he is now making application to be a janitor at the Westport United Baptist Church. ":What the heck, I need a job. I am living below the poverty level now."Our of 227 eligible voters, 189 ballots were cast and three were spoiled according to returning officer, Eileen Brinton.

On March 21,1990, the following letter appeared in The Digby Courier, signed by Laforest G. Norwood.

Dear Editor: This score from the Brier Island Coliseum: Christians 97, Lions 89.

Now that the electorate of the village of Westport has voted to remain free of the sale of alcoholic beverages, I hope this same electorate will take the next logical step and free our Christian village of bootleggers. It can't be done by secret ballot.

All the above was written by me, is my opinion and is not quoted from another person.

In 1993, the vote was taken again. This time Islanders agreed the Village would be "wet."

First Moose! Alva McDormand of Westport shot this 920 pound moose near Wreck Cove, Cape Breton . Her name was one of 200 picked in a Provincial moose draw . Mrs. McDormand, age 60, said this was the first moose she'd ever killed. The spread from antler to antler on the 23 point head dress is four feet. The moose dressed out at 740 pounds. Mrs. MDormand and her husband, Charlie said they have their winter meat supply now. (Oct. 8, 1986) Photo courtesy Alva McDormand.

Lodge and Dining Room Open
June 6, 1990

Brier Island Lodge opened June 4 in Westport. The facility features a dining room with a seating capacity for 50 and 10 guest rooms . The Lodge is of log construction and is located on the highest point of land on Brier Island. An Open House will be held at the new facility on Thursday, June 7, from 2-4 p.m.

The view from the 30 ft.glass solarium in the dining room or from the deck outside includes the village of Freeport, Grand Passage,Peter's Island Light, St. Mary's Bay and the French Shore. At night the lights of Yarmouth can be seen.

Brier Island Lodge is owned and operated by Ray and Virginia Tudor. Mr.Tudor said he decided to built the Lodge because "we realized in 1988 there seemed to be a greater influx of visitors to Brier Island all the time. It was all built on location. We had many comments on the location.

"We are very aware of the fact that eco-tourism is coming into its own. This is nature-based and from what better location?" Mr. Tudor commented.

Last summer, Mr. and Mrs. Tudor operated a Bed and Breakfast from their home which is located adjacent to the Lodge."Everyone we spoke with about the idea of a Lodge and dining room was very supportive. The common thread, people from literally all over the world came together in their enchantment and their appreciation of Brier Island. One lady said,'You people live in a post card here.'" Mr. Tudor recalled.

He said he and his wife began trying to put together a financing package "to realize our goals of a lodge at this particular location. Then we went from there.

"For Brier Island,the high profile attraction is whales. But we also realize we have a very unique location here. It's many things to many people. Some are interested just in the peace and quiet. We have just a gravel road going by here which ends at the lighthouse. The only sounds which might intrude upon the silence are the fog horns.

"It will always be nature-based because Nature Conservancy owns half the island. That's the beauty of it, it's not going to change," he added.Mr. Tudor said they will be offering guided nature tours along the rugged coastline of the island and also through the interior. The tour guide will also offer historical information about the island. They plan to hold mystery weekends in the fall and arts and crafts seminars.

There is a gift shop at the Lodge featuring work by local crafts people.In addition to offering a service for visitors, Mr. Tudor said the facility is for the community, "designed and thought of with the community in mind."

The dining room at the Lodge has a seating capacity for 60. Fresh local seafood will be featured on the menu. Mr. Tudor said a specialty menu will be offered beginning in July. They also plan clambakes and lobster boils on the shore.

Mr. Tudor said they will cater to weddings and other private parties. The Lodge and dining room are completely accessible to the handicapped. One guest room is designed especially for the handicapped. Two of the rooms have whirlpool baths. Each room is decorated in a different decor. Some are designated non-smoking as is a part of the dining area.

The facility was built by Acadian Log Home of Plympton. There are 14 full and part-time employees at the Lodge and dining room, including the owners.

An aerial view of Brier Island Lodge in 1994 showing the many additions to the original structure. Photo by Thomas E. Norwood

Though there is no police presence on Brier Island, people tend to live law-abiding lives. Occasionally there are car accidents. Usually the occupants are unhurt.

A truck driven by Ricky Buckman failed to make the turn off Wellington Street. The truck hit Grace Frost's house, causing considerable damage. No one was injured.

David Buckman walked away from this spectacular mishap which occured in February, 1991 near The Bridge.

Stephen Welch was not injured when his went too close to a shop near the Robicheau's store. This photo was taken in July, 1980.

Malida Swift was slightly injured when her car went off the Government wharf while she was waiting to get on the ferry. Shown examining the car are Irma and Jimmy Swift. March 15, 1988.

261

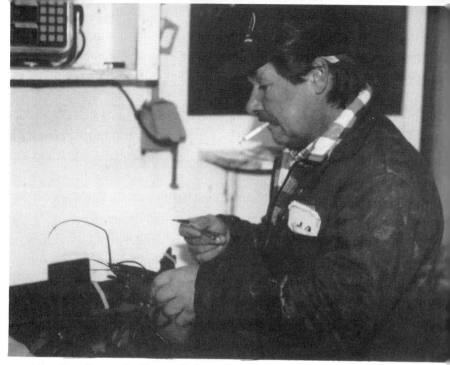

A familiar face at the Kenney Lobster Pound. In the winter, Dale Elliott works with lobsters.

In the summer, Dale can be found working on lobster crates across from the Pound or doing other maintenance.

The younger generation wait for the Annual Westport Days parade to begin. ____
Photo taken in 1991   Photo by Thomas E. Norwood

Westport head commissioner Gordon Thompson gets some help from
Thomas Norwood, l. and David Buckman, r. as he puts up a new sign
welcoming people to Westport. September, 1980.

The Theme Remains the Same
Graduation in a Small Island School
July 4,1984

There were six people in the graduating class at Islands Consolidated School in Freeport this year. The stage in the old gym was decorated with white paper flowers and red crepe paper strips. Someone had made the letters "ICS" out of white flowers. This was in front of the podium.Two baskets of lupine brought colour to either end of the stage. Some metal chairs had been placed up there and a table stood in front of the microphone.

Young children, dressed in their finest, ran around among the milling adults as the Island residents waited for the ceremony to begin at 7.Outside, a few people were having a last minute smoke. "Did you see Harry How on the ferry when you crossed the Passage," someone inquired as new arrivals walked past."No, he wasn't on that ferry," came the reply. This meant the guest speaker, Chief Judge of the Provincial Magistrate Court couldn't make it until the next ferry at least.

At precisely 7:03, the energetic Principal of ICS, David Rolls, strode to the microphone and asked the graduates to line up in the back of the gym. Helen Welch, retired teacher from Westport, took her place at the piano and began playing the traditional "March of the Priests."

Everyone stood up to watch the six young people file past in their red gowns and mortarboards. Some adults stood outside the crowd to snap pictures.

Mr. Rolls announced the guest speaker had missed the ferry in East Ferry. He wouldn't be on hand to speak at the appointed time."If we're all agreed, we'll go ahead with our program and fit Judge How in when he gets here, are we agreed?" Mr. Rolls asked."I'm not hearing any dissent so I guess we're agreed," he laughed. "Let's all sing O Canada, everybody sing," he exclaimed.

Everyone sang. The anthem was a bit muffled in the middle because some people sang the old words while the more informed sang the new version. The traditional graduation ceremony that was being enacted in countless high schools across North America began in Freeport at this small rural school. There was an opening Prayer, followed by a speech by Mr. Rolls. He said it would be brief, and it was.

He told the graduates to determine their options and choose those that would help them grow. He cautioned them not to forget their roots. "Schooling is a small box of tools and with it, you are now going to have to build the rest of your life," he advised.Mr. Rolls told the graduates to seek happiness rather than materiel wealth. "Remember, you only get out of life what you put into it Don't be afraid of hard work," he concluded.

Michael Langley, principal of Digby Elementary School spoke about the importance of having encouragement during the learning process.He said the graduates would need encouragement in whatever endeavors they take up next. "We learn through a process of trial and error," he noted.

The ceremony continued with granting of diplomas to the graduates. First came the three gentlemen: Earl Crocker, Greg Peters and Neil Tibert. Though not a member of the graduating class, Mark Nichols was called to the stage to receive a Grade 12 diploma.Mr. Rolls shook hands with the graduates as he gave them the rolled certificates.Next came the ladies: Sherri Outhouse, Jackie Outhouse and Angela Elliott each stepped forward for their diplomas. They not only got a handshake, they each got a hug, much to the delight of the audience.

Awards were presented by Ed Donovaro and Mr. Rolls. Mr. Rolls noted another of the honoured guests, Warden Wilfred Swift had not yet arrived.As is the case in so many graduations, one or two students picked up many awards. Neil Tibert seemed to garner the lion's share of trophies and bursaries. There were special awards for those missing the least number of school days and a Library Award to the person who helped most in the library.

There were two memorial trophies which are given every year in memory of cousins who died in individual accidents in their teens. The audience was quiet during the preliminary announcement but cheered when the recipients were announced. A relative of the two young men was called forward on each occasion to make the presentation.Another memorial trophy was presented by a widow of the former school janitor. The audience clapped warmly as she made her way to the stage.

Mr. Rolls said he noticed Warden Swift in the back of the room. "Would you like to come up and take your place on the stage?" he asked.He also announced he had just received word that Judge How had caught the 7:30 ferry and was, at that very moment, making his way across the Island.

The ceremony continued with more awards. Then Judge How came forward. He was introduced by Mr. Donovaro as the Chief Justice of the Supreme Court of Nova Scotia. No one noticed Judge How's promotion. He later called this newspaper to note his correct title.Judge How apologized for being late but noted this was not an uncommon occurrence for him. he said he was a bit relieved to learn Warden Swift had arrived late also.

Warden Swift said he'd been ready in plenty of time but thought the graduation started at 8 p.m.By the time Judge How began to speak, the younger children had begun to fidget and turn in their seats. They talked and laughed while adults listened intently to Judge How's message. There were more awards, more pictures taken, more cheers.

The hit of the evening was the class history read by graduate Earl Crocker. Obviously ill at ease, the young man smiled and made his way through the written report. He traced his class through their beginning in 1971 until the present, noting who had joined the class each year and who had left. He wiped his brow on several occasions and laughed along with the audience when he fumbled a word or lost his place.The graduates filed out to Mrs. Welch's piano notes. More picture taking words of congratulations, then it was all over.

There were no large monetary awards or scholarships; no band music; no print programs; no large roster of distinguished guests.But the graduates have a night to remember when they were honoured by their family, friends and teachers, who helped them along the way to their grade 12 graduation.

The graduating class of 1984 at Islands Consolidated School, Freeport. L. to r. Angela Elliott, Sherri Outhouse, Jackie Outhouse, Greg Peters, Neil Tibert and Earl Crocker.

Old Schools Still Stand
February 20, 1980

The three old schools on Long and Brier Islands have been closed for many years. Today they have one thing in common: a lack of window glass. All are privately owned now and not being used except for storage.

The school in Westport was built about 1910. It housed students from grade primary to 12 at one time, later to grade 11. There were four large classrooms with a wide central stairway. Each room had a coal stove in the center, tended by the teacher.   "You either kept the stove going or you froze," was the way former teacher Etta Webber described the situation.Mrs. Webber taught in the old school for many years. She said it was always cold and drafty in the winter. She also recalls the wide plank floors as being difficult to keep clean.

The present Westport School opened in 1962 for grades primary through eight. Junior high and high school students went across to Freeport to the new Islands Consolidated School.

The late Victor Strickland purchased the old school shortly after it was closed. He used the building for storage and had a workshop in one of the downstairs rooms. Last year the building was sold to Nathan Kadan, an American. Mr. Kadan's plans for the building are not known.

The old school in Tiverton was built about 70 years ago, according to one estimate. Ruth Outhouse taught the lower grades in the school shortly before it was closed. She said primary to grade five classes were held in the two rooms downstairs, grades 6 through 11 were in the two rooms upstairs.

Mrs. Outhouse said she couldn't recall the school being "terribly cold," but does believe modern plumbing would have been an asset in the building. She said at the time the school was closed, many parents were not happy about sending the younger students down the island to nearby Freeport.

"People in Tiverton felt they were going to keep their school for grades primary through six. But all of a sudden, they realized it was all over. They hadn't attended the right meetings and then it was too late,"she concluded.

Grafton Outhouse owns the building now. He went to school in the two-storey structure. His future plans for the cavernous building? "None to report at this time."

Florence Tibert of Freeport taught in the former Freeport school. She said only three rooms were in use when she taught there. The building had been in bad shape for some time before it was closed, she recalled.

She said there was a fourth room which had been used at one time. Helen Welch of Westport remembered they prepared this fourth classroom when she went to teach at the old Freeport school. She believes the extra room was used to handle students coming from Central Grove.

The junior and senior high students transferred to the present Islands Consolidated School, a short distance from the old school. The first section of this new school was completed 18 years ago. An elementary wing was added four years later, according to Keith Manzer, principal of the school. Elementary students continued to attend the old Freeport School until the new wing was completed.

Mansell Quartermain, vice-president of Finance for Connor Brothers, Ltd. said his company owns the old Freeport school though they do not use it at present. Connor Brothers owns a fish plant in Freeport. They have not opened the plant for the past two summers but when they were using it, they used the old school to store paper supplies.

Mrs. Tibert said there is a fourth island school which is also closed. This is the one-room school in Central Grove. It is owned by Theodore Buckman and has been used as a garage in past years. Mrs. Tibert said she taught there four years, grades 1-11. One year there were 43 pupils. The school closed once in 1940, re-opened for the 1946-47 school year. After that, Central Grove students went to either Freeport or Tiverton

Westport children sang at the official opening of the Westport Library. The author led the singing and is shown at left. Photo by Janet Denton

The old school in Westport before it was repaired by the present owner,
Nathan Kadan.

The Westport School, 1979

Who Owns the Hearse?
May 7, 1980

There is a stately, black horse-drawn hearse reposing amidst dust and cobwebs in the Hearse House behind the Baptist Church here. The hand-crafted hearse features fringed leather curtains and curved glass panels. It is minus three wooden-spoked wheels and one glass window is broken but it is definitely restorable.

Rev. David Roy, pastor of the Church, said he believes the three missing wheels are stored in the Church basement. He said they were removed by concerned parishioners because the hearse was being taken on unscheduled trips each Halloween.

Etta Webber, treasurer of the Church, said the Halloween capers were not the cause of the broken glass. "That damage has occurred in recent years while the hearse was in that building." Mrs. Webber said she does not know who owns the hearse, though she suggested it might belong to the Village.As far as I know, it always sat up there and everybody used it. Not matter who died, they used it."

Helen Bailey, who is 85 years old, agreed with Mrs. Webber. "Members of both the Church of Christ and the Baptist Church used that hearse," she said. She remembers seeing it drawn by a horse followed by a large procession of mourners proceeding up the dirt road to the cemetery at the top of the hill. Mrs. Bailey said the hearse was used up until the mid-1930's. Two people who drove the hearse during the last years it was used were Allen Moore and Ed Pugh.

Wallis Gower, another octogenarian, recalled the hearse being used when he was a young boy. "It was a very serious situation when someone died. Everyone went to the funeral," he said. "That hearse was feared by us young people."

It caused more than fear when it was used as a Halloween prank during the 1950's and 1960's. Mrs. Webber said the hearse was frequently left in the yard of an older resident. This created amusement for the prankster but exasperated the householder.

No one seems to know when the hearse was brought to Brier Island. Mrs. Bailey believes it was purchased in Yarmouth.

271

The hearse remains stored behind the Baptist Church.

The Westport Hearse as it was in 1980, stored behind the Baptist Church.

Bird Banding Ongoing Project
June 11, 1980

A 32-acre plot of land here near Northern Point was the scene of organized activity punctuated by cries of delight recently. People approached a canvas shelter bearing brown paper bags. They would announce triumphantly, "From Alder II, a black-throated green warbler, female": or "Got a good female Blackburnian warbler from Green Net I." A young man, followed by an eager group of young people, bounded into the shelter with a white cloth bag, "From North Point II, a male Redstart," he announced.

Sitting calmly amidst a pile of empty paper and cloth bags was amateur ornithologist, Ross Anderson. He would carefully extract each fluttering bird from the bag, examine it for identifying marks, then place a tiny, aluminum band around one leg. Occasionally he would point out some unique feature of the bird to the group gathered around him. Then he would balance the bird on one finger for a moment. Finally, it would fly away, usually to perch in a nearby spruce tree where it could be watched some more by the birders.

"This is the fifth year we have been doing this study," Mr. Anderson commented. He is working on a bird banding project with the North American Bird Banding Association. "I am carrying out a migration study of small passerines," he revealed. The passerines include more than half of all living song birds and consist mainly of altricial songbirds of perching habits.

Mr. Anderson said Acadia University has owned this land since the early 1960's. It was donated to Acadia by Willet Mills, Halifax, who wanted the land used for wildlife study.This is the only place on the island where the banding operation is carried out. "The potential up here is so vast, we just don't have the time or manpower to go anywhere else on the island," Mr. Anderson noted.

He was assisted this spring by his wife, Mary; several young Westport residents and Carolyn Crawford Smith. Mrs. Smith's husband, Dr. Peter Smith, is an ornithologist and biology professor at Acadia. He was away at Bon Portage Island, off Shag Harbour, constructing a shelter for future bird banding expeditions there."This is the first year there have been so many young people interested in the project. They have been a great help," Mr. Anderson smiled, adding, "They can come here as much as they want."

Nylon mist nets are set up in various spots on the property. The birds fly into the slender netting and become entangled. There were only 13 nets set up here this spring because there was not enough manpower available to check more than that number frequently.

"If we don't check the nets frequently, the birds will tangle up and possibly hurt themselves. Also there is a chance a sharp-shinned hawk will grab them out of the net," Mrs. Smith said.

Sometimes they catch a bird that has already been banded a short while before. They have also caught birds that were banded here last fall. The highlight of this spring banding expedition was catching a Western Tanager, an extremely rare bird in this part of North America.

In identifying the birds, Mr. Anderson sometimes refers to a Bird Banders Guide put out by Penn State Univ. This provides a key to identifying selective birds. "If you can't identify a bird, you can't band it," he noted.

They have banded about 90 species of birds here since the project began. "There have been over 350 species of birds seen in Nova Scotia. I would say we are looking at banding probably 120-130 different species here," he added.

Mr. Anderson said the license to band birds is issued by the Dept. of Canadian Wildlife Service. "You have to have a specific study you want to carry out and be certified by two professional ornithologists," he explained. His license states he is allowed to band passerines and waterfowl.

They do not catch many large birds in the mist nets. "The largest we have caught around here would be the sharp-shinned hawk which is about two-thirds the size of a crow," Mrs. Smith said. They do catch hummingbirds but do not band them."They have a special size band, we have to let them go," Mrs. Smith said.

Ornithologist G. Stuart Keith recently commented that "birders in the old days used to be portrayed by cartoonists as guys with pith helmets and knobby knees or as little old ladies in tennis shoes." On this island, the bird watcher might be a housewife or lighthouse keeper. Increasingly, it is the young generation who can be seen walking with binoculars and bird guide. This increased awareness in birds on this official migration spot is directly related to Mr. Anderson and the Acadia University staff who have encouraged participation in their project.

Amateur Ornithologist, Ross Anderson bands a black-throated green warbler at the banding station set up near Northern Point. Several young Westport residents watched the procedure intently. l. to r. are Ronnie Denton, Mitchell Swift, Lisa Wood, Thomas Norwood, Charles Buckman and Susanna Norwood. June, 1980

NSPC Predicts Better Service for Islands
Jan. 14, 1981

The zone manager for Nova Scotia Power Corporation says electric service to Long and Brier Islands will "steadily improve" as the NSPC institutes $1.5 million worth of repairs and new installations to the 65 kilometer transmission line from Digby.

Albert Fulton met with village commissioners from Westport, Freeport and Tiverton to discuss the need for a qualified linesman based on either island.

Gordon Thompson, Westport head commissioner had written to the NSPC as well as the Board of Public Utilities, outlining the Islands' needs for a linesman.

Mr. Fulton said the considerable expense involved in stationing a linesman, plus equipment on the Islands prohibits such a move by the utility.He further pointed out that this linesman, if stationed on the Islands, would be required to work in Digby during the day as there would not be enough work on the Islands to keep one or two qualified people busy.

"So you would still be without a linesman half the time should an emergency occur," he said.The village commissioners had cited their worry about electrical problems occurring during storms when ferry service to the mainland is not possible. They also voiced concern about cutting off electricity to burning buildings.

Mr. Fulton said the situation on the Islands is no different from that of many isolated rural communities.He added if the Corporation stationed linesmen on these Islands, they would be forced to provide the same service to other islands in Nova Scotia. "This cost would be enormous."

He asked the commissioners to give the utility a chance to verify their improvements in equipment and transmission lines will eliminate problems faced in past years.In addition to putting in new transmission lines, the NSPC is also planning a new sub-station in East Ferry. Surges in voltage experienced in the past should be totally eliminated. "By spring, voltage problems should be pretty well rectified."

The World of Westports held their annual convention in Westport, Nova Scotia in August, 1992. This truck was decorated for the parade by the Super Seniors group.

The wind blew so hard on March 13, 1993 that this mobile home was flipped from it s location on cider blocks and placed neatly several feet away. The mobile has since been moved to a new location across from the Baptist Church.

Randy Bezant playing basketball on the edge of Water Street, summer, 1981.

Those Who Work Beyond the
Call of Duty Deserve Our Thanks
November 29, 1989

We were a bit smug on this side of the Bay early last week. Those of us listening to Saint John radio stations on Nov. 21 heard about terrible driving conditions, heavy snowfall, strong winds, etc. in New Brunswick. But on this side of the Bay, it was just rain. That is until early afternoon. Then the rain changed to snow.

I was in Hassett on Highway 340 at the moment when raindrops turned to thick, pelting snowflakes. I had just interviewed Colonel Sullivan and his wife, Dorothy. The three of us struggled against the wind and snow to get a photo of the Sullivans with a coyote he'd shot.

Then I started for home. Driving slowly, very slowly, I arrived at East Ferry at 5:15 p.m. I saw the red and green lights of a boat far out in the Passage, nearly in St. Mary's Bay. I thought it must be a dragger coming in but then decided it was the ferry Joshua Slocum It was still light enough to see the boat at that time.

I checked with some people from Westport waiting in line ahead of me to find out what was going on. They said the ferry had gone down the Passage to wait until the tide slacked a bit. They estimated the wait at one to two hours.

I waited nearly an hour. It was dark,cold and snowing hard. The car was being buffeted by strong gusts of wind. I decided it might be more sensible to drive back to Digby. I got out of the lineup but as soon as I got the car turned around, I decided against the idea. I met a wall of swirling snow. The thought of going down Sandy Cove hill sideways crossed my mind.

I got back in the lineup and made a nest out of two coats I had in the car. I figured it was better to huddle in my car than risk the tortuous drive back to Digby. I was half asleep when I heard engines revving and vehicles moving. It was 6:15 and the ferry was in. What a pleasant sight!

Though it was very rough, we made the crossing without incident and landed with hardly a bump on the other side. Another slippery-sliding drive to Freeport and, of course, the ferry was not there. I got the coats organized again and waited over half an hour until the Westport ferry came in. Several times vehicles would drive up and shine their headlights at the wildly tossing waves on the ferry slip. It seemed impossible that the ferry could land under such conditions but it did.

During the wait in Freeport, the electricity flickered, then went out altogether. Westport was also in darkness. Power was out for some 10 hours on the islands. The next day, I learned the Nova Scotia Power Corp. crews had worked their regular shift on Tuesday, then stayed onto work throughout the night to restore power.

Many others involved i n public service stayed on the job that night, going without proper rest and working in severe weather conditions.I have great admiration for the captains and crews aboard those ferries that night who continued to provide service so people could get to their homes. The captain has complete responsibility of the ferry and must make the decision whether or not to attempt a crossing.

I also appreciate the NSPC crews who risked their own lives so others could wake up in warm homes with electricity to power their many conveniences the next day. So often we take these services for granted and are just vaguely aware of those who perform them. These are dedicated people who definitely deserve our thanks.

The Westport branch of the Scotiabank. For many years, this bank operated every Thursday afternoon from 1-4 in this former fish plant office. The bankers, money and pertinent papers arrived in Westport on the 1 p.m. ferry. The bank closed permanently April 29, 1993.

Betty Shea presents a clock to the Westport Public Library. Her father, Ralph Gould made this clock and a similar one which he gave to the Westport School. Mr. Gould is a resident of Cape Elizabeth, Maine. He has made substantial contributions to the Westport Library since its inception two years ago. August, 1980

Fish plant workers crossing to Westport on the Petite Passage II in 1982.

Who Took the "Tom Cat Alley" Sign?
June 18, 1986

Someone has taken the Tom Cat Alley sign from a telephone pole inn Westport.It's not really a crisis situation but it is puzzling to the Village Commissioners.

A few weeks ago, the Commissioners had signs placed at the intersections of all the Village streets, lanes and roads. Head Commissioner Gordon Thompson said the signs were made some time ago by a Katimavik group. Mr. Thompson said he carefully researched the proper name for each road, using an 1864 map and other historical data.

One narrow roadway leading from front road to the back road was designated Tom Cat Alley. Mr. Thompson said this road has been called Tom Cat Alley for as long as anyone can remember.
The "Tom Cat Alley" sign was placed prominently, some 15 feet up on a telephone pole at the intersection on Water Street. Two weeks later, the sign disappeared.

Mr. Thompson said he doesn't think it was a youthful prank. He said he heard rumours some of those living on or near Tom Cat Alley were not pleased with the name. He has another Tom Cat Alley sign which he's going to put a at the intersection but this time, he plans to nail it in a less prominent position. It will be placed on the former Westport Co-op store situated at the intersection.

Mr. Thompson said he's heard two versions as to how the road got its name. He said Tom Cat Alley started as just a cart path, a short cut for people wishing to get from the front road to the back road. At one time, there were thick spruce trees lining the road and several houses which were situated very close to the edge of the road. Mr. Thompsons aid apparently tom cats did frequent the area.

Over the years, the spruce trees have been cut down, several of the houses torn down, the street paved and maintained by the Dept. of Transportation.Some have suggested Tom Cat Lane might be amore dignified name.Mr. Thompson said he thinks the authentic, original name should stay, adding to the charm of this island village.

Meanwhile, Villagers are wondering just who has the Tom Cat alley sign and when, if ever, will it surface again?

Post Script: After this article appeared in the Digby Courier, a letter was sent to the editor about the sign and about "strangers" moving into a community and causing trouble. A letter was also sent to Mr. Thompson. It read as follows:

Gordon Thompson: The name Tom Cat Alley came from a Hoar House head of this Lane, and now long gone and torn down. We all don't like the name on our land or in our neighborhood. There should be a much more uplifting name for this Lane. We are taxpayers and should have some say. Please do not put up such a degrading sign. How would you like the sign on your property?

Gordon Thompson replied: I am not responsible for the naming of Tom Cat Alley; however, I am responsible for putting the sign up. If you want the name erased from the books, please go through the proper channels which would be to go to a ratepayers' meeting and have the ratepayers vote on the matter or else get up a petition with 20 names on it, indicating their objection to the name, and present it to the Commissioners, which would lead to a ratepayers' meeting anyway.

Until such time as this is done, there will be another sign put up, bearing the same name.Back came another letter from the irate homeowner:, this one again going to the Courier editor.

We hope you have a good time with your paper, which we have canceled. You can put the sign up if it pleases you. It shows what respect we have from all of you.

Then Gordon Thompson wrote a Letter to the Editor:

In response to the letter in your paper of July 2 with regards to the name, "Tom Cat Alley," if the writer wants the name changed, why does he not go through the regular channels and attend Village meetings so that such matters could be looked after properly?

Derogatory remarks such as there being a whorehouse on Tom Cat Alley many years ago are resented because most of us were of the understanding that the name came from there being a great number of tom cats living on the lane (the meowing kind).

Now, thanks to the letter writer, the whole world has been enlightened on the breed of tomcat that was busy there in the late 1800's.By placing the sign, we did not intend to start a controversy, but it appears one person is in disagreement - the vast majority find the name amusing and it is indeed a very pretty lane.

Everyone in the Village is not of the same opinion of "strangers" coming to live in Westport as a great many of them have contributed in positive ways to the life of the Village. Signed: Gordon Thompson, Head Commissioner

And finally, I wrote an editorial titled:When Does a Resident Cease to be a "Stranger"?

A letter to the editor this week comments about "strangers" moving into communities and causing trouble. The letter writer, in this case, is referring to the editor and her family who moved to Westport ten years ago.

Too often we hear unfavorable comments from longtime residents about"strangers" who move into a community and quickly begin to take part in local government or civic groups. Too often, these newcomers are resented by those whose forefathers lived in the community for some years past.

One could easily argue that we are all residents of a fairly large community called Canada and we are newcomers at birth. Though our ancestors may have lived in a community for generations, each individual stars a new life,to be based on his or her own merits.

From our experience, we have found newcomers to a community frequently bring new enthusiasm and new ideas to sometimes sagging organizations. Many times, it is the new residents in town who are most active in civic or sports organizations. it is not uncommon to find a "stranger" starting the historical society in a community, assuming positions of responsibility with the volunteer fire department or volunteering to help at a local hospital.

"Strangers" who have lived in other areas bring a different viewpoint to their new community because of their varied experiences.Traditions die hard and some say a family must live in a community for several generations before being accepted as one of the "locals' and not a "stranger." According to the Scriptures, Jesus was a stranger in every town he visited.

We would hope most longtime residents in this area will continue to welcome newcomers into their communities. In the long run, we will all benefit.

This is Tom Cat Alley. This quiet village lane has become the subject of some controversy in Westport. (July, 1986)

In Westport

New Restaurant Opens

June, 1989

A new restaurant with 30-seat dining room opened on Brier Island, June 15. Located on Second Street, in Westport, the restaurant is an addition to the Westport Inn Bed and Breakfast.

The Westport Inn and Restaurant is owned by Nancy and Rollie Swift. The couple opened their bed and breakfast four years ago in a century-old house originally owned by Mrs. Swift's grandparents.

Mrs. Swift said she had often thought about opening a restaurant because she felt there was a real need for such a service in Westport. "The reason we initially thought about it was because when our guests would call for a booking, they would ask if there was any place to eat. Last year, we had over 500 guests in our house. They all asked if I would feed them. At that time, I was working fulltime as a bookkeeper. I figured I might just as well open this restaurant and do the one job," Mrs. Swift said.

The restaurant is open Monday through Thursday from 6 a.m.until 9 p.m. and on Friday, Saturday and Sunday from 6 a.m. until 11 p.m. "or later if someone wants to eat," Mrs. Swift added.

She said her own day begins at 5:30 a.m. when she starts making her famous Brier Island Buns which are served throughout the day in several ways. The restaurant offers a Whale Watcher's Special; Brier Island Burger and a Bird Watcher's Special, sandwiches all served on Brier Island Buns. Mrs. Swift also makes all rolls, deserts and soups served throughout the day.

The restaurant offers complete take-out service and will prepare box lunches. Mrs. Swift said the variety of foods offered on the menu was partially suggested by their son, Roland, who is a long-distance trucker. "He has eaten in restaurants all over North America. He drives for All Cities American. He helped us a great deal with the menu," she noted.

Though neither Mr. or Mrs. Swift have had previous experience operating a restaurant, Mrs. Swift pointed out she has had a great deal of experience cooking for her family which includes four grown children and for her friends.

Mr. Swift's father, the late Wilfred Swift at one time operated a restaurant on the waterfront in Westport. It was called "Foof's Place." The Building washed away during the Groundhog Storm of 1976.

"Rollie's father always used to tell us 'Somebody should start a restaurant,'" Mrs. Swift recalled. The couple is assisted at the restaurant by their daughter , Coralee Sollows and by Lana Titus.

For those who would like to just have a place to rest or get in out of bad weather, the Swifts have created a spacious 25 ft. by 25 ft. lounge on the third level of the restaurant building.

Mrs. Swifrt said those waiting for seating or people visiting the island, perhaps to go whale or bird watching, are welcome to use the lounge. The couple also offer a chandlery service for residents, yachtsmen or campers offering basic food items, film, crafts and brass gifts. Mrs. Swift and Mrs. Sollows make all the crafts offered at the restaurant and chandlery.

Nancy Swift in the Westport Inn. The restaurant and general store opened in June, 1989. Mrs. Swift operates the business with her husband, Rollie. The couple also have a Bed and Breakfast.

Acknowledgements

I am grateful to those who shared their stories with me. Also thanks to the many people who loaned me photos or helped me with facts and figures. I could never have put this book together without the help of so many others. Thanks to my family, who helped identify photos; my son, Nelson, who sent the required software; and son Thomas, who took so many of the photos shown in this book. He helped record the Island way of life as it was in the '80's.

About

the Author

The author was a reporter/photographer for the Maine Sunday Telegram and Portland (Maine) Press Herald for nine years and editor of The Digby Courier for seven years. She wrote and published **Life on the Tusket Islands** in 1994.